REALLY Useful Job Search Tactics

A HANDBOOK OF CONTEMPORARY JOB HUNTING TECHNIQUES

Barbara Thank you for support! Rich

by RIC

Note for Librarians: a cataloguing record for this book that includes Dewey Decimal Classification and US Library of Congress numbers is available from the Library and Archives of Canada. The complete cataloguing record can be obtained from their online database at: www.collectionscanada.ca/amicus/index-e.html

ISBN 1-4251-0574-2

Printed in Victoria, BC, Canada

Printed on paper with minimum 30% recycled fibre. Trafford's print shop runs on "green energy" from solar, wind and other environmentally-friendly power sources.

PUBLISHING™

Offices in Canada, USA, Ireland and UK

Book sales for North America and international:
Trafford Publishing, 6E–2333 Government St.,
Victoria, BC v8t 4p4 CANADA
phone 250 383 6864 (toll-free 1 888 232 4444)
fax 250 383 6804; email to orders@trafford.com

Book sales in Europe:
Trafford Publishing (uk) Ltd., Enterprise House, Wistaston Road Business Centre,
Wistaston Road, Crewe, Cheshire cw2 7rp UNITED KINGDOM
phone 01270 251 396 (local rate 0845 230 9601)
facsimile 01270 254 983; orders.uk@trafford.com

Order online at:
trafford.com/06-2332

10 9 8 7 6 5 4 3

To the Job Seeker.

Rick Gillis:
REALLY Useful Job Search Tactics

CONTENTS

Rick Gillis:
REALLY Useful Job Search Tactics

INTRODUCTION

Welcome to REALLY Useful Job Search Tactics

There are hundreds of long, involved books on job searching with much more detail than <u>Rick Gillis: REALLY Useful Job Search Tactics</u>. There are books devoted to resumes, interviews, thank you notes and every other component of the job search. They contain excellent information and you should read them if you believe they will benefit you.

I consider a lot of these books more academic than helpful. There is not much information in <u>REALLY Useful Job Search Tactics</u> that would be considered "academic" --no studies, no graphs, and no statistical backgrounds - but I assure you, academics will embrace the information that you currently hold in your hand to help them find *their* next job. That is because this is real-world stuff that you will be able to apply to your job search—right now!

***

For your benefit, a little background on me.

I have been "there." And I hope you *haven't* been "there"—but the reality is that a lot of us have. "There" is employment terminated.

I tell you this only because I want you to understand that I know personally the *"shock and awe"* that comes along with an employment termination. If this is why you have picked up REALLY Useful Job Search Tactics, I applaud your initiative. This book will do for you what no seminar, counselor or friend will do: we (you and I) will get to the core of what it is going to take for you to land your next job.

Internalize my mantra (you will see it again and again): **Make Me Money or Save Me Money**™. That statement is the basis of my live presentation, my radio show and this book. When you take ownership of this idea you will be better than 70% prepared to seek out your next employment opportunity.

Make Me Money or Save Me Money. This statement is simple—so deceptively simple—that very few people ever get it. Read this book and *you* will.

ENTRY-LEVEL JOB SEARCH

Should you happen to be an entry-level job seeker, REALLY Useful Job Search Tactics will benefit you in ways you will not appreciate at this time. I would ask you to study the concepts, apply them, and in a couple of years come back and reread this book. See if the ideas contained in here don't remain true, viable, and helpful to your career.

CURRENTLY EMPLOYED

If you are employed but want to keep your eyes on the prize, I strongly advise you to read REALLY Useful Job Search Tactics. You NEED this information. You are the job seeker everyone is looking for: the *passive* job seeker (vs. the *active* job seeker who is not currently employed). You require, at the very least, the information in Chapter 4 about keywords, resume screening systems and applicant tracking systems. The future is now. By reading this book you will enhance your climb up the career ladder. My basic tenet, Make Me Money or Save Me Money, applies equally to you.

WHERE "Make Me Money/Save Me Money" CAME FROM

I applied for my first "real" job when I was 19 years old. Prior to that I had worked in the family hardware store from the third grade. I grew up in the family business.

After my family sold the store, I found my way down to the nearby lumberyard and filled out an application. I waited my turn for an interview (such as it was for a job of that type at that time) with a whole bunch of older guys. During my interview, I vividly recall telling the lumberyard VP "for every dollar he paid me I would give him back 10". What you need to know is that I was a 19-year-old, long-haired, 125-pound, skinny-as-a–junkyard-dog, runt of a kid telling this successful businessman that, fundamentally, I understood it was going to cost him money to put me to work. After he peeled his eyebrow off the ceiling (that's what most made the impression that remains with me today), he gave me the once over, tossed me a leather pair of work gloves and a hardhat and told me to report in the next morning. I have used that same technique ever since (although the $'s have increased along the way!). Now you know *one* of the reasons why I say that I have been creating <u>REALLY Useful Job Search Tactics</u> for better than 30 years.

I genuinely and sincerely wish you the very best in your job-hunting adventure - and it just might become an adventure before it's over (It's in the retelling, after all.). Once again, internalize my mantra, apply the techniques you are about to learn and you will find yourself creating a compelling and memorable persona—you!

To Your Success!
Rick Gillis
2006

PS If after reading this book you have any REALLY Useful Job Search Tactics you would like to share, visit ***www.rickgillis.com*** and send them along. I hope to hear from you.

WHY IS ANYONE GOING TO GIVE *YOU* A JOB?

"The world doesn't pay you for what you know;
it pays you for what you do."
- Jack Canfield, The Success Principle

There is only one reason anyone will hire you: MONEY. You may *believe* you will be hired for your experience, proficiency, skills and credentials, but that will only get you an interview. You will be hired for one reason alone: you can convince a prospective employer that you will

MAKE THE COMPANY MONEY OR SAVE THE COMPANY MONEY™

Learn this first lesson well. Commit it to memory. Internalize it. Own it. Make it your daily mantra during your job search and in every interview. I know it sounds obvious, but almost all job seekers overlook it entirely. By concentrating on this one powerful statement, you will set yourself head and shoulders above the competition.

The secret to the power of this statement is that it is not about you. It is about what you can do for THEM, which is what managers want to hear: that you will **make them money or save them money**. This statement can singularly make the difference in your winning the job over other candidates.

In the following chapters, I will show you how to include this statement in your resume, your telephone pitches and interviews in ways that will catapult you to the top of the list of potential candidates. You will learn to speak the language of hiring managers and be able, when you have finished this book, to convince them that you understand THEIR problems and know how to help them increase their bottom line.

✔ WORKING IN NON-PROFIT SECTOR

Non-profits, government and social service jobs,
as well as some medical and research positions, don't
fit neatly into the "Save Money/Make Money"
definition.

No Problem. Just change your mantra to
PROVIDE ADDED VALUE OR SAVE TIME.
In seeking this kind of work, the same principles
I will teach you in this book apply equally well.

I cannot state strongly enough the advantage you gain over others with this kind of presentation. Most job candidates don't understand or, don't take into consideration in applying for work, how much it costs an employer, every day, to open his doors. It is not just employee salaries. It is also rent, utilities, insurance, maintenance of space and equipment, and employee benefits, the last of which averages about 30 percent of each employee's base salary. Plus, there are additional costs associated with non-revenue generating departments such as accounting, human resources and the administrative staff.

All must be paid before a company can show a profit, which is the reason they are in business. It takes a lot of money to hire you and to keep you around, but that is also where your value as an employee lies. When you can convince a prospective employer that you will **make or save him money** over and above his costs, you increase your value over other candidates and you increase your prospects of being hired.

With downsizing, outsourcing and "off-shoring," we live and work in a brutally competitive job market. Companies are ruthless in trimming costs, as they must be. But if you can show that you will contribute to that bottom line, your services will always have value.

HOW TO TELL INTERVIEWERS YOU WILL MAKE OR SAVE THEM MONEY

If you are looking for a revenue-generating position – that is, if you are a salesperson - it is obvious how you will make money for a company. You show a prospective employer your past production quotas and sales goals and how you stacked up against them. It's all in the numbers.

For the rest of us, it isn't as obvious at first, but that's why REALLY Useful Job Search Tactics is here. You will learn how to shape your resume and your answers to interview questions with the **make you money/ save you money** techniques. And you will be surprised at how much you can control the interview when you provide compelling, provocative answers based on your experience and good sense-answers that make you stand out from the crowd.

In the following chapters, you will learn to artfully and easily convey to potential employers your understanding that your presence costs them money and that you are therefore going to save them money. First, the basics:

- Being on time
- Doing your job well
- Finding ways to increase efficiency
- Offering new ideas to save or make money

- Being open to constructive criticism
- Taking initiative

I know. This list sounds self-evident, but even though tardiness, laziness, and lack of forethought or initiative cost companies millions of dollars every year (of course, we know that doesn't describe you!), these basics are almost never addressed in interviews – which is why you should mention them. These items can make the small difference that sets you apart from other qualified candidates and more importantly, this "little stuff" helps ease the conversation into the important stuff – your work history.

TALLY THE "LITTLE STUFF"

Keep a running tally, a diary of the times you've
gone the extra mile on your job that you may not
have been recognized for.

If you haven't done this in the past, do it now
from memory. It will be useful as I help you prepare
for interviews, and after you get the job, it will be
invaluable for annual reviews.

You will also be surprised at how much you actually
do in the course of a year that is above and
beyond the call of duty.

The most important way you will convince an employer that you can **make them money or save them money** is in presenting your past achievements and accomplishments in that context. That you showed up and did what was assigned to you is important, but it is not nearly enough. You must convey in your resume and to the interviewer how you can speed business along, slow it down when necessary, improve processes, find new applications for old equipment, and create new product ideas.

You must be able to clearly state – brag about - how you have saved past employers' money. Do this, and you will always be employable. Yes, I know, this is a new approach you haven't used before and you don't know exactly how to do it. By the end of this book, you will. I have never left an interview without saying something like, "You give me this job and I will return to you $100 or better for every dollar you pay me." It works. Keep reading and you, too, will gain the confidence to make that statement.

But first, you must memorize this lesson. Internalize it and make it your own.

REALLY Useful Job Search Tactic #1:

FROM THIS MOMENT FORWARD I WILL INTERNALIZE MY PERSONAL JOB SEARCH MANTRA: "I AM GOING TO MAKE YOU MONEY/I AM GOING TO SAVE YOU MONEY."

THE SUPERIOR RESUME™—FORMAT BASICS

*"There is nothing so easy to learn
as experience and nothing so hard to apply."*
- Josh Billings

Let me ask you a question: Based on your current resume only, would *you* hire *you*? Probably not. My goal is for you to create a resume that is *so* compelling to a reader that they know if they don't hire you, you may potentially become formidable competition for them somewhere down the road. I want an employer to create a place for you on his or her staff even if they don't have room right now. Sound daunting? It's not.

For many reasons that I won't bore you with here, I have taken it upon myself to create a new resume format. Of course it has all the parts, pieces, and considerations of the 'traditional' and 'functional' resumes but I have put a lot of thought into this format and I am proud to present you with what I call **The Superior Resume™** format.

Remember that your resume is your single most important job search tool and it serves only one purpose: to get you the interview—on the telephone or in person. It creates dialogue. It is common ground for you and the recruiter, the jumping-off place from which you will wow him or her with your knowledge, character, charm and creativity.

Once again, looking at your current resume, surely you must recognize that a list of previous employers names, job titles and lists of responsibilities won't get you in the door. I am willing to bet that your current resume more resembles an **obituary** than a forward-thinking, progressive and vital description of who you are and what you offer. This is what is fundamentally wrong with all the resume formats that you and I have been taught to use all these many years.

Your resume has to clearly spotlight your accomplishments and achievements, be compatible with current hiring technologies (much more on this later) and, this being the key difference between the **Superior Resume**™ format and all others, *announce in no uncertain terms what you are going to do for your future employer.* Welcome to the resume that not only looks back but also looks forward. Neat concept, huh?

THE 30-SECOND RULE:
YOUR RESUME WILL ONLY GET 5 TO 30 SECONDS OF REVIEW

In fact, chances are high that your resume will not be seen by a real human person at all unless it conforms to the requirements of the company's resume screening system, databases, search terms and keywords used by today's human resources professionals.

Scary. But there is no need to worry. It's not as hard as it sounds and I will walk you through each step of the process along the way.

In the previous chapter I told you to memorize and internalize your personal job search motto: make you money/save you money—that no one will hire you for any other reason. By the time you have finished these first four chapters you will have a Superior Resume that will fast-track you to the interview where you can then prove your personal mantra to the recruiter.

ACCOMPLISHMENTS AND ACHIEVEMENTS

In this chapter, we are not going to worry about the appearance and layout of your resume. We have work to do first. Work that you will appreciate because you are going to learn a lot about yourself along the way. We need to first create the content that will compel your reader to call you—the content that will make you stand out from your competition.

You will do this differently than you have in the past. This is not just a list of previous employers and your responsibilities on each job, but the accomplishments and achievements of which you are exceptionally proud - items that you can knowledgeably discuss and expand on in an interview that will hold the recruiter's attention and create a lasting impression. It's time for you to brag about yourself! *There is no time for modesty or humility during a job search.* In order to be compelling, you have no choice but to brag on yourself. This may go against your grain but deal with it. You can do it.

How do you create compelling achievements for your resume? A good question and one we must spend some time with.

Keep your resume nearby and bring out a new sheet of paper. On this page, create a list of 8 to 10 of your proudest, most memorable personal accomplishments. They don't necessarily have to be business related but for the purpose of your resume, as much as possible, they should be.

Can't think of any? Start with your resume (it's nearby, right?) and copy those points you felt were most important when you first created that document. Now ask family, friends, and particularly, co-workers what they remember most about your personal achievements.

Many times family, especially kids, will remember stuff that you haven't thought of in years. Moms are a great source of accomplishments— even if she may not know what you *really* do on the job - because moms, regardless of your history, always remember the high points you have told them over the years about your career!

Keep in mind that what you were doing as a daily, expected part of your job may, in the mind of a hiring manager, actually be an accomplishment.

I had an occasion recently to work with a boring resume that belonged to a really great guy. David's resume was boring simply because he was a payroll clerk and it didn't have any 'snap'—it didn't tell me what a great job he was capable of. After speaking with him and asking about specific accomplishments, I learned that he had processed his first payroll for 6000 employees at a major energy firm with zero returns. Now to David, he was just doing his job. But to a hiring manager do you know what kind of value (make me money/save me money!) David represented? My point is this: doing what you were supposed to be doing and doing it well may rate as an accomplishment in its own right.

CREATING AN ACHIEVEMENT

Just like a good book, a song, or movie, an accomplishment has a beginning, a middle, and an end. So does a well-crafted statement of achievement.

Take one of the accomplishments that you have listed in your existing resume.

- Example: *I was responsible for 49% of all sales for fiscal year XX.*

This is the Beginning of your accomplishment.

Now, create the Middle by just adding these two words: "RESULTING IN". (These two words are magic!)

- Example: *I was responsible for 49% of all sales for fiscal year XX RESULTING IN...*

Finally, make your accomplishment compelling by adding the Ending or, in other words, complete the sentence.

- Example: *I was responsible for 49% of all sales for fiscal year XX resulting in a contribution to net revenue in excess of $2,250,000.*

Can you see how powerful this statement is to a potential business owner, hiring manager or supervisor? This is the basis for creating a resume that is so compelling that, should I pass on you as an employee,

I risk allowing you to become my competition. You must remember your audience when writing your resume and you must remember to express to them how you have previously made employers money or saved employers money.

I mentioned earlier in this chapter that I propose a forward-looking resume. Creating such powerful and compelling achievements effectively does this (along with another critical concept you will see in the next chapter). If you will remember the audience you are preparing your resume for, keep in mind that they not only want to make or save money, they *must* make, or save, money. When an employer reads the example above, the only thing that will be going through their mind is: "I want this person to do that for *me*"! That is when you become memorable—head and shoulders above the competition.

SELLING YOURSELF IN YOUR RESUME

Your resume is your sales tool to recruiters and the language you choose to use matters. You must write in the lingo of your business—that is, the words and phrases used within your industry that tell hiring managers you know and understand your craft or business. These *keywords* (and/or phrases) will become *search terms* when you submit your resume electronically. As you are creating your accomplishments and achievements, include these specialized terms and I will discuss their very specific importance later in the Superior Electronic Resume chapter.

***

We are all human and at times, thinking we are giving ourselves an advantage, we are tempted to inflate, if not outright lie, about our accomplishments. Let me state this unequivocally: never misrepresent yourself on your resume. Today, due to liability and litigation risks, background checks and previous employment reference verifications are standard procedure for most all companies before hiring a new employee. If any embellishment or falsification is found out, you're done.

But that doesn't mean you can't "sell" yourself. Have you ever seen a job posting identifying the company as an average business with a lousy pay plan wanting to hire great people to do great things? No way! They "sell" themselves: "An aggressive, dynamic company with an exceptional compensation plan is seeking..."

You can do this too.

Let's say you are confident that you are capable of managing up to 60 employees, but you have never managed more than 15. So, say that in your resume: "I am confident and capable of managing a workforce of up to 60 people." This is what I call a "defensible statement" (not to be confused with the legal term), particularly if previous supervisors would agree. Not a misrepresentation – a statement that speaks to your future worth.

So now, go back through this new resume you are building and toot your horn some more.

QUANTIFY, QUANTIFY, QUANTIFY

Nothing sells like cold, hard numbers. One of the most powerful tools you can use is to quantify your past employment experience by expressing your achievements in percentages (%) and dollar signs ($). Here's an example:

> "During my tenure with ABC&D Company, I increased sales by 27% in my region to a record level of $2,300,000 per quarter net revenue."

Now *that* is a persuasive resume statement. Numbers and symbols always leap off the page.

Not every kind of work lends itself to this tactic, but if yours does, it's a compelling approach that can't help but lead the interviewer to ask, "How did you do that?" And then you are into a real conversation that shows how knowledgeable and creative you are about your business or industry.

Now, take a break from reading for a moment and review your

resume for any place you can insert dollar signs and percentages.

PERSONAL INFORMATION

Education

Unless you have recently graduated from high school or college, there is no reason whatever to take up valuable "real estate" at the top of your resume with an educational listing. Save it for the bottom of the page. Even if you have recently added "Masters Degree" to your resume, save it for the bottom of the page.

If, on the other hand, you have just recently graduated and are in search of an entry-level position, hold that thought until you get to the Superior Entry-Level Resume chapter. (Don't go skipping over there yet! There is still too much information here for you to work through.)

Do, however, list college degrees - the names of institutions and the degrees earned but no date—particularly for mature job seekers but also, younger job seekers may want to think about not listing dates in order to get the interview.

Military

If you served in the military, note that you were discharged and from which service - but not when. The date is not relevant. Save it for the interview...if it even comes up. If you have recently been separated from the service you will, obviously, list your military experience in your employment history and in your accomplishments as appropriate—dates and all.

References

None. Nada. No way do you put references on a resume regardless of the level of your job search. List them neatly on a separate piece of paper to have with you on interviews in the event you are asked for them, and have them at the ready to include on your formal application.

Older Job Seekers

Age discrimination is illegal in the United States but it is a fact of life in the workplace, and particularly in the job search. It is not unknown for older job seekers to be rejected solely on their age rather than for lack of qualifications, so I recommend that if you are older than 50, list no more than the last 20 years or so of work experience. I will discuss this at greater length and detail in a later chapter.

Smoking Policies

Due to insurance costs, medical considerations and potential lawsuits from non-smoking employees, many companies have instituted no-smoking jobsite policies. This is legal and a company's choice, so if you smoke, deal with it.

In addition, some companies now require, as a condition of employment, a signed statement that you do not smoke anywhere – on or off the job. If you are a non-smoker, it could tip the scale in your favor to list "non-smoker" at the top of your resume.

***

And now, you have assembled the basics you need to create your Superior Resume. You have thought through your most important accomplishments and achievements, sketched them out in a manner that includes the lingo of your business or industry and toots your own horn. If you can quantify these achievements, you've included dollar signs and percentages, and you have a list of the personal information that will round out your resume.

Next, we will tackle the REALLY Useful Job Search Tactics Superior Resume style and layout for the resume you will need, including some tricks, tactics and techniques that will put your resume above the crowd.

☆☆☆☆☆☆☆

REALLY Useful Job Search Tactic #2:

MAKE YOUR RESUME COMPELLING BY SPEAKING TO YOUR ACCOMPLISHMENTS AND ACHIEVEMENTS. DO NOT BE SHY: SELL YOURSELF!

REALLY Useful Job Search Tactic #3:

PRACTICE AND CREATE REALLY COMPELLING ACCOMPLISHMENTS BY USING THE "RESULTING IN" TECHNIQUE.

REALLY Useful Job Search Tactic #4:

USE $ SIGNS AND % SYMBOLS TO MAKE YOUR ACCOMPLISHMENTS LEAP OFF THE PAGE.

THE SUPERIOR RESUME™—THE PAPER FORMAT

"If we could sell our experiences for what they cost us,
we'd all be millionaires."
- Abigail Van Buren

In the last chapter, I presented the **Superior Resume**™ format you must master to win in a competitive job market. The electronic resume (which will be explained in the next chapter) is similar and only slightly modified (there will be *some* changes) from your paper resume. By the end of this chapter, you will have an elegant, Superior Resume™ that will make employers sit up and pay attention to you. Guaranteed!

TYPE FONT AND SPELLING

Every computer word processing program comes with a spellchecker and a grammar checker, so there is no excuse for anything but an error-free resume - and trust me - you *will* be graded. One misspelled word or typo and your resume goes straight in the can. So when you are finished creating your paper resume, run the spell checker, the grammar checker and to be extra certain, have a friend – a second pair of eyes – read your resume for any of these elementary errors.

Choose an easy-to-read font in 10- or 12-point type. You cannot go wrong with the standard Times Roman, Verdana or Arial. Don't get fancy and do not use a script font – it will work against you.

Now we are ready to format your resume.

NAME AND CONTACT INFORMATION

You determine the layout of your contact information—centered, justify left, justify right - not really all that important as long as it looks professional. But I very seriously want to talk about how much information you will place in your contact information. All you need is your name, an email address and a phone number - maybe two numbers if you want to include your landline or cell phone. But that's it. With the advent of identity theft and all the ways you can be identified from information *you* provide online and in person, I strongly recommend that you resist including your physical address on your resume. If you are not willing to relocate, you may want to include your city or town but that's it. Do not provide any information on your resume other than what is required to help you find a job. This advice applies to your in-hand, paper resume and especially to your electronic resume.

Of interest as well is the fact that your home street address at the top of your resume could work against you. Recruiters regularly eliminate candidates who live where a long commute would be involved.

Back to relocation - if you are willing to relocate, then state it clearly at the top of your resume. Just a short note, —"Willing to relocate"—on one side will do it. This is also a good place to post "Non smoker", if applicable.

The last piece of information that you may want to add to the header of your resume is your personal web address. We will discuss this in much more detail later in the book, but it is my belief that one day, instead of sending resumes via snail mail or email, we will be forwarding the link to our personal job seeking website. A well-identified link is more likely to be opened versus an attachment, which some companies will not open due to fear of viruses. The natural place to note this on your resume would obviously be along with your email address.

SAMPLE RESUME HEADER

Jerry Job Seeker	
jjseeker@personalemailaddress	Home: (212) 123.4567
www.j&jseekerpersonalwebaddress.com	Cell: (212) 123.4568
Willing to Relocate	Non Smoker

A note here about email addresses. If you have been using a cute or fun address like hotdude@abc&d.com, you'll need a new one. You can set up a free, online email service at such places as Yahoo! or Gmail. I recommend that you put your name in your new address: janesmith@abc&d.com. If someone else already has that email address, you can attach a number at the end so it may look like this: janesmith3@abc&d.com.

YOUR "SEEKING STATEMENT™"

What follows is one of the singularly most important pieces of information you will learn in REALLY Useful Job Search Tactics. This one sentence on your resume could result in it being read or ignored - **The Seeking Statement**™. You really have no idea how much this sentence pleases recruiters and hiring managers at all levels—simply because nobody uses one.

And guess what? **The Seeking Statement**™ does exactly what it says—it tells your reader what position you want. Crazy simple!

I am seeking a position as a Fashion Merchandising Coordinator.
That's it! State exactly what position you are seeking. One line. Direct. Sweet!

In the not too recent past, it was very common for a job seeker to submit a resume with the idea that someone (a real person!) would actually take the time to read his or her resume and think—"Voila! I know where we can use this person"! Well, forget it. Unless you are applying to a smaller shop or business, those days are long gone.

I have been promoting my **Seeking Statement**™ for years with the reasoning that you should make it easy for your interviewer to know exactly what position you are applying for. And also to make sure your resume would get passed on to someone with authority by someone who has none and probably does not know what the heck all that information below the contact information means!

It turns out that this advice was not only good but also prescient. The new reality is that in February of 2006 the Department of Labor, Employment Standards Administration issued a ruling that will eventually apply to all companies that employ 50 or more people. This rule is called the <u>Obligation To Solicit Race and Gender Data for Agency Enforcement</u> and is further described as <u>The New OFCCP (Office of Federal Contract Compliance Programs) Internet Applicant Recordkeeping</u>. I won't go into all the specifics here (the ruling is 19 pages long and you can visit *www. dol.gov/esa/ofccp* and search 'Internet Applicant' for *all* the details—if you really want to) but, from a job seeker point of view, finding a job online has recently gotten more difficult. The gist of the rule is this: you, as an online job seeker (I know, I'm jumping ahead of myself since we will cover the online resume in the next chapter—but this is important and appropriate here as well), are required to declare an "expression of interest" in an online position or your resume DOES NOT HAVE TO BE CONSIDERED BY THE EMPLOYER who is in receipt of your electronic resume. How does that apply to this discussion? Your Seeking Statement is *exactly* the right vehicle to declare your specific interest in every position for which you submit your resume and at the same time ensure that you are not removed from consideration under this rule.

Here is the kicker. You have to state the title of the position precisely as it appears in the posting. If you find an employment posting on a job board for a "Human Resources Senior Recruiter" and you submit your resume as a "Human Resources Recruiter" - you do NOT have to be considered for the position. Now, you very well may be considered but the employer does not *have* to do so per this ruling.

It has been estimated that the Human Resources department will be obligated to spend 5 hours a month on additional recordkeeping in order to be in compliance with this ruling. Do you really think they will accept any marginal resume they can refuse when they know they will be required to audit that resume?!

One more consideration for your Seeking Statement - you may want to add the job reference number if one is listed and you may even want to include the name of the company in your Seeking Statement.

SAMPLE SEEKING STATEMENT

> **I am seeking a position as Manager of Internet Sales, Reference #D723, with Giant Internet Sales Company.**

Remember that your resume only gets 5 to 30 seconds of review. Give your readers the information they most want at the top of your resume. If you are answering an ad, use the exact job title they listed online or in the newspaper and your resume will be reviewed.

YOUR OBJECTIVE STATEMENT

In Chapter 2, I said that most resumes resemble an obituary. I stand by this - they only speak to the past.

The REALLY Useful Job Search Tactics Superior Resume is a *forward-looking* resume. You must express to your *future* employer how you will make or save them money, and what better place to do that on your resume than in your Objective Statement?

I recently had the opportunity to discuss this idea with a retired Director of Staffing for one of the largest energy companies in the world. I asked him how many times, during his 33 years as a Human Resources professional, someone he interviewed had stated in-person or in-resume, that he or she was there to "add shareholder value" to the organization. You can guess what his answer was: "Never". This is astonishing to me!

Let's change that—you and me. Let's make your Objective Statement speak to the value you are bringing to your future employer.

SAMPLE OBJECTIVE STATEMENT

OBJECTIVE STATEMENT
As Manager of Internet Sales for Giant Internet Sales Company, I will significantly increase net revenue by implementation of current management and motivational techniques acquired through previous experience and continuing managerial education.

Do you recognize how sweet and simple this statement is? In just one sentence Jerry Job Seeker has clearly stated his objective for his future employer. He is writing with his audience in mind. Tell your future employer what they want (and should expect) to hear.

THE SUPERIOR RESUME™ "TWO WINDOWS" FORMAT

This section is important. It is where REALLY Useful Job Search Tactics again departs from almost all other resume advice. Standard resumes list jobs with a sentence or two about responsibilities performed on the job. They all look alike, they all read alike and none tells the interviewer what makes the candidate special. But the goal of REALLY Useful Job Search Tactics is to show you how to separate yourself from the crowd. The "Two Windows" style of resume will:

- Place you head-and-shoulders above equally talented and educated people
- Boldly and confidently state your personal accomplishments and achievements
- Define you and your abilities no matter what your age
- Most importantly, *compel* the reader to contact you

To do this, you are going to divide the next two components of your resume into two windows:

WINDOW 1: Accomplishments and Achievements

WINDOW 2: Your Employment History

Treat these "Windows" as two entirely separate sections of your resume.

In Window 1, you will list only those accomplishments of which you are most proud, NOT in chronological order, but in order of greatest achievement.

In Window 2, you will list your employment history timeline in chronological order, most recent first, as in standard resumes but with less information than you are used to providing in traditional resumes.

What you accomplish with my "Two Windows" format is to emphasize up front your top achievements while still listing those all-important places of employment that recruiters need to see.

***

Let me take a minute to explain the concept behind the REALLY Useful Job Search Tactics Two Windows resume format. Imagine you are standing inside your house looking out the front window. You have a view. Now turn around and look out your back window. You have a completely different view, but they both come from inside the same house.

Think of your career as your employment "house". The view out your front window is your achievements and accomplishments; the view out the back window is your employment history. Houses for sale are first noticed because of curb appeal. Let's sell you based on your curb appeal - your accomplishments.

WINDOW # 1

Let's begin by looking at your work sheet of eight to ten accomplishments (or more) that you have recently created. By now, in each description, you should have pointed out how you made previous employers money or saved them money and you have quantified your achievements where possible using the *"resulting in"* tactic described in CREATING AN ACHIEVEMENT in Chapter 2. Remember, not all achievements of this stature need to be money/dollar oriented (think charitable events, volunteer efforts, family, etc.) but most can be described with some dollar orientation attached and this will make them more "attractive" to an employer.

Now, go through those achievements, select the four or five or, maximum - six of which you are most proud and order them, not chronologically, but from most outstanding at the top to "least" outstanding at the bottom. These are what you will include in Window #1 under the header, Selected Personal Achievements. Remember, you list no dates, no titles and no company names. Just achievements.

Window # 1: SAMPLE SELECTED PERSONAL ACHIEVEMENTS

SELECTED PERSONAL ACHIEVEMENTS

•Inherited and then overcame a $5,000,000 deficit in a badly designed national sales promotion by completely redesigning and developing a far superior plan resulting in a new system that reduced typical man-hours the sales staff devoted to plan by 23% while increasing sales in excess of $1,300,000 per quarter.

•Saved over $500,000 annually in key sales communication systems and national transportation expenses while improving level of service to clientele.

•Dramatically reduced sales staff turnover by 28% due to a more focused recruiting and selection process. Enhanced training and the creation of targeted management groups resulted in countless man-hour savings.

You may ask why "selected" achievements? Because those listed are not *all* you have to be proud of. When your recruiter calls in person, because of your work sheet, you will confidently state that those are only the "top 5". Also, when a recruiter calls and asks how you did such-and-such, respond with just enough information to set your listener on edge and then, seek out a natural stopping point, and state, matter of factly, that you look forward to telling them more—"in person", "in their office", or "out of the office for coffee". Try to take control of the situation and gain some personal leverage if possible.

* * *

Once again, I want to point out that dates, company names and titles are not as important as the achievements themselves. Do you see how the dollar signs ($) and percentage symbols (%) jump off the page? Did you notice that I did not say $1.3 million but rather $1,300,000— with all the zero's "spelled out"? This is powerful! Whole numbers (not abbreviations) attract attention (make me money/save me money) and will jump off a page. It is necessary that you knock the socks off the person who is reading your resume and compel them to read on.

My goal for you and your resume is to become *SO* compelling to an employer that they *must* call you, thereby creating a dialogue. Ultimately, between your resume and your in-person interview, where you will confidently discuss your accomplishments and achievements, I want you to become *so* compelling to your interviewer that they will literally become concerned about letting you slip through their fingers. You must clearly state (because you have overcome all modesty at this point!) that should this employer *not* hire you, they (once again and worth repeating!) run the very real possibility that they will soon cross paths with you—but as the competition! I want your very next employer to determine, even if they don't currently have the time, space, or budget to bring you (and your abilities to make or save them money) on board, they will *create* that space for you.

WINDOW #2

Now that you have floored your readers with your achievements, it is time to tell them where you did all this wonderful work. But, you will NOT tie your professional achievements to the companies where you accomplished them. In this way, you create a reason for the reader to telephone. Remember, the sole purpose of your resume is to get an appointment. And you want the reader of your resume to meet this highly accomplished person—you!

Below your <u>Selected Personal Achievements</u>, you will list your places of employment for the past 20 years (plus or minus) in Window #2. Assuming you have the history, try to keep it to no more than 20 years, although you must be prepared to discuss any prior work as it comes up in interviews.

Begin with the header, <u>Employment History</u>, and then follow this layout for each company where you worked:

Company Name, City, State   **Dates Employed**
    Your Job Title While There
What the company does (i.e. makes, manufactures, sells, etc.)

Notice again that you explain only what the company does, not what *you* did while you worked there. You have already told them about you in Window #1 - your Selected Personal Achievements. Now let them try to figure out where you did all those marvelous things.

Window #2: SAMPLE EMPLOYMENT HISTORY

EMPLOYMENT HISTORY

Giant National Employment Web Site, Atlanta, GA Jan 2002-Present
  Director, West Coast Sales
Giant National Employment Web Site is recognized as one of the leading employment websites worldwide.

Gulf Coast Group Internet, Houston, TX   1998-2001
  Sales Manager, South Central US
Texas-based Gulf Coast Group is one of the nation's leading providers of employment Internet-related solutions such as resume screening services & applicant tracking systems.

The Express Internet Company, New Orleans, LA   1997-1998
  Employment Internet Startup Consultant
The Express Company, currently operating profitably in 27 markets in 13 states, offers turnkey Internet services from web design to network applications with a staff of 33 employees.

With the REALLY Useful Job Search Tactics Superior Resume format, your outstanding achievements are always listed right up front on the first page where they grab your readers' attention. And always keep in mind that *the top half of the first page of your resume* is the single most important part of your resume. Hook them here and you will have them reading the entire document.

***

AN INTERESTING COMMENT ON THIS FORMAT
A person who had attended one of my speaking engagements and had submitted his resume in the Superior Resume format to several

companies recently approached me. He was concerned because a recruiter had called saying that she "needed more information" from him since his resume seemed to be "limited". I asked what the problem was. *She had called him!* Someone interested in what he had to offer had created a dialogue. This is exactly the result I want you to have when using this format.

Also of importance, I believe, is the elegant appearance of the Superior Resume format. One page—maybe a little bit more. Clean. Packed with highly relevant information. And you are available to provide the rest in person!

EDUCATION, MILITARY SERVICE, HONORS & AWARDS

In Chapter 2, you made note of your education and military service and now you add this information below your employment history. Do not include dates of graduation or military discharge. They serve no purpose—unless of course, you just got out of the service and then you need to be presenting your military service within the "Two Windows" and not here.

Under the header, **Education**, list college degrees and any classes or certifications that will set you apart from other job seekers. This is particularly important for Information Technology professionals (See Chapter 5). Sometimes the list of certifications and classes is lengthy. If you feel they are relevant and worthy, list them. If not, don't fill up the page with them.

Honors and Awards can be a sticky subject. Sticky because you may want to list them but, ask yourself, do they really have any value on your resume? Some people have a knack for knowing exactly which honor to list and how. Others (not you, of course) are comfortable listing awards that have very little value—except to them and a previous company. If you question the value of an award, it is probably best not to list it. Regardless, keep these listings to the barest minimum possible.

SELECTED KEYWORDS

In the next chapter we will be discussing keywords and search terms extensively. For the purpose of formatting your resume now, understand that, due to the advent of resume screening software, you will likely *not* have all the words in your resume that may be searched for to determine if your resume rates a "human" review. It is now very common and acceptable to include a category called <u>Selected Keywords</u> at the bottom/end of your resume and you need to plan on creating a running list of these words. This may be a new idea for you to consider but it is necessary in view of the technologies being applied to most resumes today.

View current employment ads on various job sites and any posting you find that has terms that could apply to you, pull those terms and phrases that you *have not already included in your resume* and list them in a continuous single line, no punctuation, single-spaced one after the other. Format these words to your heart's desire but style here is not nearly as important as content.

We will discuss these keywords in much more detail in the next chapter. For now, accept that they are a required element of your resume and place them here. You will be very pleased that you did!

SAMPLE SELECTED KEYWORDS for Jerry Job Seeker

<u>**SELECTED KEYWORDS**</u>
Sales marketing advertising networking consumer retention consumer survey website development website sales Internet sales return on investment promotional campaign

***

A special note to job seekers older than 50: Unfortunately, age discrimination is a fact of life in the job market, and even though it is illegal, it is virtually impossible to prove. (We will address this in much more detail in Chapter 12). With that in mind, there is no reason to use dates that serve no purpose but to reveal your age. Is it really important to your resume that you graduated from college in 1972? The answer is an emphatic "NO". What is important is that you own the degree. That's all you need to say.

Remember, the purpose of your resume is to get the appointment, create the dialogue. That done, you will dazzle them with your achievements and capabilities, and with the Superior Resume format, interviewers will have all kinds of questions for you. That's when you will tell them what it was like overcoming a $5,000,000 promotional deficit.

***

Now, it is time to check your finished resume for spelling and grammar. When you are confident that it is letter perfect, there is one final item to consider: printing. As sensational as the content of your resume is, it needs to look attractive, too. When recruiters and interviewers are sorting through hundreds of resumes, neatness counts, and a professionally laid-out resume will leap to their attention.

A margin of one inch on all four sides is standard. Proper spacing between sections, appropriate bolding and underlining and bullet points will make your resume easy to read. Choose an ivory or white, high-grade paper that is heavier than the usual computer printer paper. 20- to 25-pound weight, available in all office supply stores, is a good choice.

Whew! You're done. In the next chapter, we will turn this paper resume into the online version you will need during your REALLY Useful Online Job Search.

REALLY Useful Job Search Tactic #5:

CREATE A POWERFUL AND SIMPLE SEEKING STATEMENT.

REALLY Useful Job Search Tactic #6:

USE YOUR OBJECTIVE STATEMENT TO SPEAK TO THE FUTURE: TELL YOUR FUTURE EMPLOYER WHAT YOU WILL BE DOING FOR THEM.

REALLY Useful Job Search Tactic #7:

CREATE POWERFUL ACCOMPLISHMENTS THAT SPEAK TO YOUR EMPLOYER BY EXPRESSING HOW YOU HAVE MADE MONEY OR SAVED MONEY FOR PREVIOUS EMPLOYERS. USE THE "RESULTING IN" TECHNIQUE TO MAKE STATEMENTS THAT ARE COMPLETE AND $ SIGNS AND % SYMBOLS AS WELL AS COMPLETELY "SPELLED OUT" NUMBERS TO MAKE THE READER'S EYE JUMP TO YOUR HIGHLIGHTS.

REALLY Useful Job Search Tactic #8:

USE SELECTED KEYWORDS AND KEY-PHRASES YOU WERE NOT ABLE TO USE IN YOUR ACCOMPLISHIMENTS OR EMPLOYMENT DESCRIPTIONS. (YOU WILL LEARN WHY IN THE NEXT CHAPTER.)

Sample Completed Superior Resume ™

Jerry Job Seeker

jjseeker@personalemailaddress Home:
j&jseekerpersonalwebaddress.com Cell:
Willing to Relocate

(212) 123.4567
(212) 123.4568
Non-Smoker

I am seeking a position as a Manager of Internet Sales, Reference #D723, with Giant Internet Sales Company.

OBJECTIVE STATEMENT

As Manager of Internet Sales for Giant Internet Sales Company, I will significantly increase net revenues by implementation of current management and motivational techniques acquired through previous experience and continuing managerial education.

SELECTED PERSONAL ACHIEVEMENTS

- Inherited and then overcame a $5,000,000 deficit in a badly designed national sales promotion by completely redesigning and developing a far superior plan resulting in a new system that reduced typical man-hours the sales staff devoted to plan by 23% while increasing sales in excess of $1,300,000 per quarter.

- Saved over $500,000 annually in key sales communication systems and national transportation expenses while improving level of service to clientele.

- Dramatically reduced sales staff turnover by 28% due to a more focused recruiting and selection process. Enhanced training and the creation of targeted management groups resulted in countless man-hour savings.

- Analyzed and merged more than 14 compensation plans into one corporate plan that resulted in savings exceeding $270,000 the following fiscal year while continuing to fairly compensate the sales staff for their efforts.

THE SUPERIOR Online RESUME & Resume Screening Systems

"The will to win is important, but the will to prepare is vital."
- Joe Paterno

Okay, you have finished the hardest work now by creating a finely tuned Superior Resume that shows a potential employer how you will **make them money or save them money**. But we do live in a brave new world and in the recent past, hiring practices have been taken over by computers. So in this chapter, I will show you how to adapt your paper resume to an online form to complement these new technologies.

Don't worry; your electronic resume will remain essentially the same as your paper version with the same content and layout. The difference is in the changes needed for the resume submission and screening process. At the end of this chapter, you will be knowledgeable in the ways of navigating the software currently in place designed to sort and file your resume into the "oblivion" archive - never to be seen again - or filed into the "forward to hiring manager" file.

NOTE:

In this chapter, I am talking about resumes submitted by email *as an attachment.*

This is *not* the same as an Online Employment Application in which you complete a form on an employer's website. Sometimes, the online application is the only method available to apply for a job and the advice in this chapter *will not work.*

If you know of a way to use these techniques in an online application, please contact me right away! - rg

BACKGROUND & DESCRIPTION OF APPLICANT TRACKING SYSTEMS & RESUME SCREENING SOFTWARE

Today, a large percentage of companies use computer programs known as Applicant Tracking Systems (ATS) to file and then search through resumes they have received. These programs were created as a direct result of the success of the internet. It does not matter if a position is posted on one of the national job sites or a local job board, the result is the same: overwhelming response to job offerings due to the world-wide nature of the web resulting in hundreds, even thousands of resumes, potentially from all over the place.

Applicant Tracking Systems organize into a database the jobs, job descriptions, the posting of jobs online, the receipt of resumes and the follow-up work required to bring an employee on board. From interview to hire thru to retirement, most systems can now track an employee's entire chronological history with an organization.

This may sound bleak and cold to you as an applicant, but the corporate world not only love these systems, they *require* them to deal with the burden of recordkeeping. The downside for you is the possibility of becoming lost in the system. It's probably happened to you: one day you are visiting one of the national job boards online and see the perfect position. It sounds like they were thinking of you personally when they wrote the job description. You submit your resume and never hear another word. Why? You wondered.

Probably because your resume lacked the necessary **keywords** or **key-phrases** required to pop your resume out of the computer when the hiring manager searched his company's ATS/Resume Screening Feature.

You will enjoy what is coming up! This is where REALLY Useful Job Search Tactics will earn its keep on your business bookshelf.

KEYWORDS—AN OVERVIEW

Keywords, also called search terms (Techies will know them as metatags), are what "fuel" the internet and any database, including resume screening systems (also known as resume filters). Mega-fortunes have been made on the web and with computer programs based on the use of keywords. Every time you go online and ask your search engine (Google, MSN, AOL, Yahoo!, etc.) to find some information for you, you are using keywords.

For example: you want to learn more about orchids. When you type in the keyword "orchid," the search engine has been given the assignment to locate every web page on the internet that contains that word. This is why your return from Google includes a statement that reads "Results 1 through 20 of about 4,383,824 for orchid." That's how many pages Google located that contain that word.

So what does this have to do with getting your electronic resume noticed? Everything!

When you submit a resume by email, it is unlikely that a real person will see it right away - especially if you have sent your resume to a generic email address such as jobs@giant&company.com. Instead, it is automatically archived in a database of a Resume Screening System where it sits with *all* the other resumes received for that job posting and, possibly, to a master database of everyone who has *ever* submitted a resume to that company.

If, on the other hand, the email address for a job posting contains a personal name or initials (jsmith@giant&company.com or janes@ giant&company.com), it is more likely a real, breathing, human person will receive your resume. It indicates a company is probably small (and that's not bad!), may not hire frequently and does it the old-fashioned way in which case, a cover letter is essential. (More on cover letters in Chapter 8.) Giant companies with generic email addresses may or may not include cover letters when they archive your resume into their databases.

Now, when the hiring manager is ready to begin interviewing, he or she will access the Resume Screening System and ask for all resumes that scored, let's say, 90% or better. That's right-a percentage grade. So if the original request in the screening system included 10 keywords, your resume must have at least 9 of them in order just to get a look! If you only have 8 you will not be receiving a call to interview. Had you known the system you could have *easily* added another 5 to 10 and made the grade!

To illustrate, let's say I am hiring for a Human Resources manager. The keywords or key phrases I require to be mentioned in all resumes before I will actually view a single piece of paper may be: employee benefits, compensation, HIPAA, HRIS, EAP, Change Management, Organizational Infrastructure, MBA, cultural processes, performance review experience, payroll.

You may not know those words or acronyms, but an HR professional most likely will and the Resume Screening System will produce only those resumes to the hiring manager that contain these words.

So you see now that including keywords in your resume is crucial to getting an interview. Think of how many talented individuals miss the cut daily simply because they don't know how to game the system! It's like tossing diamonds into the street.

Okay, you say, but you still haven't told me how to use them to help my resume get noticed. You're right, but I thought you needed to know the *why* before the *how*. Now here's the scoop for your electronic resume.

KEYWORD RECOGNITION TACTICS

In the previous chapters, I showed you how to include the "lingo" – the keywords of your industry – in your resume. "Isn't that enough?" you may ask. Well, yes. And that's good. But what if you were not able to insert *all* the keywords a hiring manager might request?

And what if you could *invisibly* insert every industry-applicable keyword into your electronic resume so they would be recognized by the computer database when the hiring manager does his search?

You can. Here's how.

Keyword Tactic No. 1: The Invisible Word List

(NOTE: The following instructions are for use in Microsoft Word, but are easily adaptable to other word processing programs.)

After the last line of your resume, skip a line and type every keyword or term you can think of that relates to your job and your industry— every one. Be certain to spell each word correctly and leave one space between each word whether it is a single word or a phrase. Do *not* use punctuation. The list for an audio engineering position may look like this:

> Microphone phantom power condenser audio recording studio audio engineering multimedia post production mastering signal processor sequencing software audio plug in

You may not know what these terms mean, but two audio engineers can throw them around with complete understanding. More importantly, the studio manager, who *will* know these terms, will search based on these keywords and those resumes that contain these terms will pop out of the Resume Screening System – *but the keywords will not be visible.* To make that happen, follow these instructions:

- With your mouse, highlight all the words you have typed in.
- Find the capital "A" with the bold underline on the Microsoft Word toolbar at the top of your computer screen. *
- This is your Font Color icon. Click the small arrow to its right.
- The Font Color palette will open and there will be several colors to choose from. Click the white square in the lower right corner.

And look at that! You have just caused the keywords you highlighted disappear. Think of it as electronic whiteout. They cannot be read on screen and they will not print. But the Resume Screening System, which will be grading your resume, *will* read them.

---

*   If the Font Color icon is not visible on your toolbar, open FORMAT in the upper left corner of your toolbar. Click on FONT and then select Font COLOR. Click the arrow and the FONT COLOR palette will open.

IMPORTANT NOTE:

Should you decide to use this technique—and every entry-level resume, at least, should - you must be certain that you have not misspelled any words because your recipient's computer will highlight misspellings with a "floating" red underscore even though the words are invisible to the reader.

For the same reason you may need to capitalize the first word in the list so a green underscore will not show indicating a capitalization error.

Keyword Tactic No. 2: Embedding the Job Posting

Here is another clever use of the whiteout technique. Copy the entire job posting at the bottom of your resume and make it invisible - with the same instructions above in Keyword Tactic No. 1 - embedding the entire job posting in the submitted resume.

This works because job postings contain many, if not all, of the keywords that the hiring manager will use to search for resumes in the Resume Screening System. In fact, there is no reason you can't list both keywords *and* copy the job description at the bottom of your resume – a sure way to be certain your resume is at or near the top of the pile.

If you are not comfortable with concealing your keywords/key phrases, I still recommend that you embed the job posting in every resume you submit.

Keyword Tactic No. 3: The Underscore Technique

Another variation involves not color, but font size. With this technique, you can reduce your keywords to appear as a line at the bottom of your resume or anywhere else you may choose to place it. (I tend to paste it under the contact information at the top of the resume creating a natural demarcation line.) To the reader it will just appear to be a line. The Resume Scanning System, however, will be reading keywords. Here is how:

- Highlight your list of perfectly spelled keywords
- Click on Format in the upper left of the Microsoft Word toolbar
- Then click Font. The Font box will open
- At the far right of the Font box, highlight the point size listed, and then type over that number/font point size with the number "1"
- Click OK at the bottom of the Font box

You have just created what looks like a line or an underscore at the end of your resume, which, to the screening system, is the complete list of your keywords, reduced to a font size that is not readable by the human eye.

Keyword Tactic No. 4: The Obvious Technique

(This is the expansion of the Selected Keywords discussion promised in Chapter 3)

Some industries, particularly the information technology guys, are aware of these techniques for concealing keywords. In fact, it was invented for the internet when websites hid keywords known to be popularly used in search engines in an attempt to rank their websites higher in the results than they would otherwise be. The search engines caught on quickly and banned the practice.

So if you work in an information technology-intensive field, you may not want to hide your keywords. In that case, create a heading at the bottom of your resume called Selected Keywords and follow it with the list of words relevant to your job search. Most fields of employment now recognize these for what they are and accept them as a legitimate addition to your resume.

What you have done in using any of these techniques is to make your resume highly "attractive" to Resume Screening Systems, which will score your resume higher than those without keywords.

FINDING THE RIGHT KEYWORDS

Every industry, every skill has its own set of keywords, the unique shorthand – the lingo – professionals use when they speak with one another. You already used some of these words when you created your print resume in the previous chapters. You will not need to repeat words already in use in the body of your resume in your keyword list. But, if you should decide not to embed the job posting, you *must* include all keywords and phrases in the job posting you are responding to that you recognize as unique.

You can improve your keyword list by searching online. I've turned up several excellent sites by searching "employment keywords," but you should be more specific than that by including your industry in the search. For example: "employment keywords manufacturing" or "employment keywords accounting".

Also, your state employment agency may have a book of such keywords listed by industry and your local library may have the same book. However, you'll save a lot of time by searching the internet.

I want to warn you about one thing: don't overdo the number of keywords you include. If you can't "walk the talk," you'll be out the door on your backside so fast you won't know what happened. No one needs that kind of embarrassment, so include only the lingo you can defend. "Defensible." Remember that concept from Chapter 2?

The point of using these keyword techniques in your electronic resume is to get noticed and get the interview. After you are in the door, you will dazzle the interviewer with your achievements, your accomplishments and how you will **save them money or make them money.**

OPTIONAL TECHNIQUE: THE ONLINE RESUME

Techies have been using online resumes for years, but they are becoming more popular and useful for all industries.

You can easily do this by using any one of the many search engine websites that offer free and very low cost personal websites. If you choose to go with a free service be aware that you will have advertising banner(s) and/or tiles on your pages. How do you think they make this service available at no cost?

My recommendation is to post your resume, any supporting documentation such as awards, honors, letters, and etc. that will verify your achievements and accomplishments and very little else. It is very easy to overdo a website, especially a personal one. DO NOT include your wife's cheesy glamour photo or that 16-pound fish you and your son caught last year. You must focus your attention on creating a very dynamic and professional first-look at you, the job seeker. After you get the job—then rock 'n' roll! (If you haven't already done so, it's probably time you learned to create your own site anyway!)

To get started, go to a major domain hosting service such as GoDaddy.com and register your domain name. Try using your own name first (ie. www.rickgillis.com) and check to verify its availability. If it is, the cost at a site like GoDaddy.com to register is less than $10 per year for a .com name and usually less for other suffixes such as .net or .org. GoDaddy specifically offers free templates and online guidance that you can use to build a personal site. Follow the various instructions on the site or call for guidance.

After creating and publishing your website (if you decide to create a personal site you will quickly come to understand what the term "publishing" means), be certain to add your link to all outgoing correspondence whether paper or electronic.

* * *

There is a lot of valuable information in this chapter and you may want to re-read it to get all you can out of it. Except for the smallest of organizations, Resume Screening Systems are so commonplace that you need to know how to "game" the system. And a note of special interest: many of the online job boards—both local and national—are now offering their customers resume screening features. Recruiters just don't want all those unqualified resumes. Can you blame them?

☆☆☆☆☆☆☆

REALLY Useful Job Search Tactic # 9:

USE THE INVISIBLE AND UNDERSCORE KEYWORDS TECHNIQUES TO GET YOUR RESUME SENT TO THE TOP OF THE PILE.

REALLY Useful Job Search Tactic #10:

COPY, PASTE AND CONCEAL (EMBED) THE JOB POSTING FOR ALL POSITIONS YOU SUBMIT YOUR RESUME.

REALLY Useful Job Search Tactic # 11:

CONSIDER CREATING A PERSONAL JOB SEEKING WEBSITE AND INCLUDING THE LINK IN ALL ONLINE AND PAPER CORRESPONDENCE.

THE SUPERIOR Information Technology Professional's RESUME

*"Innovation distinguishes between
a leader and a follower."*
- Steve Jobs

Why, you may ask, is a chapter just for information technology (IT) professionals necessary? Because many IT professionals need it.

There was a time, up until about 2003, when the "new economy" - the internet, e-commerce, abundant venture capital and the IPO investment bubble - was so desperate for your talents and there were so few of you that you were paid like rock stars. In those days, you spent as much of your workday fielding recruiter inquiries as you did writing code. The IT world was your oyster.

No more. For more than a decade now, universities and technical schools have been graduating students expert in every conceivable IT course the schools could think up. Simultaneously, corporations have been outsourcing their IT needs to offshore where IT labor is less expensive. The bottom line for you is that the supply of IT workers has been outstripping demand.

Still, it's not all bad news. The "herd" is beginning to thin as IT professionals move into other fields, but the days of the easy big bucks, ponytails and Dr. Seuss T-shirts at the office are pretty much gone. The

IT pro must become part of the business team, contributing to and meeting the goals of company management.

Today you must compete in the same manner as the "civilian" workforce just to get your resume noticed. And like job seekers in any other specialty, you must be able to show potential employers that you can **save them money or make them money**.

If you are an IT professional who skipped straight to this chapter, stop now and go back to read *Chapter 1 – WHY IS ANYONE GOING TO GIVE YOU A JOB* and *Chapter 4 – THE SUPERIOR Electronic RESUME & Resume Filtering Systems*. You need to know the basics of the innovative Superior Resume first, and then I will explain the tweaks that apply to IT pros only.

INFORMATION TECHNOLOGY RESUME TWEAKS

Your IT resume includes all the essentials of "civilian" resumes in the same format and order as the sample at the end of Chapter Three - including the Seeking Statement at the top. A lot of the information in IT resumes is Greek to the average Joe or Josephine recruiter assigned to fill the position, so don't make it hard for them to figure out what you do. State the name of the job you are seeking in the same words a company department head or manager is likely to have specified it for the recruiter. Help them match you to the title.

QUANTIFY YOUR IT ACHIEVEMENTS

Some of the most powerful advice in this book is how to show recruiters and potential employers how you will **make them money or save them money**. Due to the nature of information technology work, that may not be as easily done as it is for sales people or managers, but you can achieve it, sometimes with dollars and percentages or with strong, defensible statements that show the business results of your professional efforts.

Following the format of the sample resume, change the name of Window #1 in the Two Windows format to <u>Notable Personal</u>

Achievements (vs. Selected Personal Achievements) and if you know how much money your work saved or made for previous employers, state it with dollar signs and/or percentage signs prominent.

If you don't have this information, contact previous employers and ask what the accumulated results of your work amounted to. They have this information because they had to justify your rock-star salary to someone. You want this for your resume because in your line of work, your contribution to the bottom line, individually or as a team member, is likely to be impressive – sometimes in the mid- or high six-figures plus, and that makes you powerfully attractive to potential employers.

With so much language in IT resumes they don't understand, recruiters are looking for reasons to throw out resumes. Don't give it to them. Use those $ and % symbols liberally when you have the facts. That's the language owners/hiring managers/recruiters speak.

When you don't have or can't locate those quantifiable results, you can still make a splash with defensible statements. Here is an example of a real-world achievement Brian, an IT professional I worked with, included after we discussed and quantified one of his more significant achievements:

> *"Successfully wrote and implemented code to enhance ATM card PIN security for European clients that resulted in significant fraud reduction and, as an unforeseen benefit to client, reduced required monthly service calls by 400 man-hours."*

Brian's original achievement/statement basically indicated that he had written 10,000 lines of code over six months, was paid for his services, and he left. After contacting that particular employer—who had to justify the money Brian was paid—he learned of the additional bonus to the company of 400 man-hours saved. Let's guesstimate that each man-hour is worth $100 (probably much more in reality) times 400 = $40,000 a month or $480,000 a year! That is quantification! And Brian now has something of real merit to discuss at interview time.

Even without numbers and symbols, Brian's statement is powerful. In the first part, Brian not only **saved them money** (fraud reduction), he **made them money** (reduced man-hours) he just hadn't told them (or himself) how much! End result? Brian ended up modifying his accomplishment to include the $480,000 figure, which made his resume really snap!

CLASSES AND CERTIFICATIONS

Follow the instructions in Chapter Three for Window #2, listing your previous places of employment, followed by your higher education and degrees. Then, you will add a section that is unnecessary to most other resumes. Call it "Additional Classes and Certifications."

In general, I advise job seekers, as much as possible, to keep their resume to one page, but in the IT world, you can forget that one – it's rarely possible. You can, however, keep it to two pages.

In this section, list all the pertinent IT classes, schools, languages and certifications you have. It is probably not necessary to add dates, but feel free to include them particularly if they relate to current and cutting edge knowledge you have recently acquired.

KEYWORDS

It is not necessary to repeat the words and key-phrases you listed in your certifications section, but if you do, be certain they are spelled exactly as they are in the first instance.

And, because IT people know all the tricks – after all, you guys *invented* them - don't bother with concealing your keywords as I advised for "civilian" resumes. List them in any order, in continuous, single-spaced lines of print - not a vertical list - to keep your resume to two pages.

The days of IT professionals being the golden boys and girls of the business world are still here. But now you must fight for your next job along with everyone else. These tweaks will make your resume more "recruiter-friendly" which will help you get the interview. Then, when you're interviewing with the IT hiring manager, you can speak the lingo of operating systems, databases, computer languages, etc. that are, quite frankly, a mystery to the rest of us.

REALLY Useful Job Search Tactic #12:

FOLLOW THE RULES OF THE "CIVILIAN" RESUME BUT DETERMINE THE VALUE YOU OF YOUR WORK ON PAST ASSIGNMENTS BY CONTACTING PREVIOUS SUPERVISORS/CONTRACTORS AND DETERMINING HOW ALL THAT CODE YOU WROTE MADE THE EMPLOYER MONEY OR SAVED THEM MONEY. USE THIS INFORMATION TO QUANTIFY YOUR SUPERIOR RESUME.

THE SUPERIOR Entry-Level RESUME

"If your ship doesn't come in, swim out to it."
- Jonathan Winters

IMPORTANT NOTE:
If you are an entry-level job seeker and you skipped straight to this chapter, stop now. Go back to the beginning; read Chapters 1 through 4. Although the examples are undoubtedly beyond your current experience, you need to understand the REALLY Useful Job Search Tactics philosophy, format and mantra before reading this chapter covering specific examples to suit your entry-level situation.

It's a story as old as employment itself: you need experience to get a job, but you can't get a job without experience.

If it's any consolation (and I know it's not), you are not the first to face this dilemma. Every working adult has gone through it, and a lot of older job seekers would be more successful today if they would stretch their memories to recall the ingenuity, spunk and creativity they applied to their first job-hunts – just like you are doing right now.

MAKE THEM MONEY/SAVE THEM MONEY

What you have in common with every job seeker older than you who is reading this book is the REALLY Useful Job Search Tactics mantra. (You *did* go back and read Chapters 1 through 4, right?) Learn it. Memorize it. Internalize it! Make it part of your being: **Make Them Money/Save Them Money**.

As powerful as that mantra is for any job seeker, it is even more powerful for a young person looking for his or her first professional job. A surly, old, heard-it-all-before hiring manager won't forget a 23-year-old who understands that it costs the company money to open its doors every morning, and expressing that idea in a job interview puts you way ahead of the ordinary young adult just out of school.

So, let's get you ready to go out and sell yourself.

SCRATCH LIST OF ACCOMPLISHMENTS

In this chapter, we assume:

- You are just out of school at any level – high school, tech school, culinary school, college, or an advanced degree
- You have a minimum amount of employment history and perhaps none

If you have more, all the better.

Start by making a scratch list to work from, a list of those things you have done in your life that you consider your personal-best accomplishments. At the beginning of this exercise, nothing is trivial - list them all: bagging groceries, flipping burgers, mowing lawns, baby-sitting, delivering newspapers.

Some are probably not work-related or for a wage. Some high-visibility examples could include high school or college athletic involvement, scholarships received, awards earned. Less visible, but important are such achievements as volunteer work or grade point averages. Right now, it all counts. Put everything you can think of on your scratch list, and then set it aside while we tackle some other issues.

RESUME FORMAT

I understand that anyone reading this who is just out of school was born with a computer mouse in hand. I know how computer savvy you are and that you have never known life without computers. But for a job search, you need to ditch your inclination to show off all the cool stuff you know about graphics and layout.

Your resume is a tool, and only a tool, to get you an interview - which is what will get you your first job. You will be marked down for anything that distracts from the hard information a hiring manager needs to know to decide to meet with you in person. Worse, fancy graphics, fonts, and shadows are likely to trash your resume when it can't be read by the company's resume screening software. So stick to the straight and narrow on resume layout.

PERSONAL INFORMATION

(If you haven't done so yet, go back and read Chapters 1 through 4. Layout for your resume is similar to that for more experienced job seekers and those chapters will provide some good detail I won't repeat here.)

Center your name in bold at the top of the page. If you are willing to relocate to another city, omit your current address (if you listed it), city, and state and indicate your willingness to move alongside your contact information. Remember, you do not need to list your current address anywhere on your resume.

Because I know you have spent most of your teen years and early 20s downloading ring tones and assorted telephone answering messages, creating outrageous email address names and posting pictures from last week's beach party on MySpace.com, let's have a serious talk about these communications devices. Even if some of you don't need it, others do.

At the top of your resume, include the telephone number at which you can be most easily found. Most likely, this is your cell phone and if that is the case, you must create a professional voice-mail message that a recruiter will actually leave a message with. "Yo, you know the drill" isn't going to get it.

The same is true for your email address. If it is not professional – and you know what I mean - get the less colorful "yourname@ freemail&domain.com" that will make you appear to be the competent adult I know you are now that your school years are done.

Although it has nothing to do with your resume itself, let us consider the internet and all the many traces you have left of yourself during the past few years in chat rooms, forums, social networking sites like MySpace, FaceBook, and, perhaps, on your own blog.

Once you get to the point of serious consideration for a professional position, the recruiter, before spending money on a background check, will "Google" your name. It is common practice now and will be done by any prospective employer. So should you.

Should you happen to be the purveyor of a website dedicated to the overthrow of Western civilization as we know it, you might want to modify your web presence before you send out your first resume. If you have posted *all* the photos from spring break in Cancun last year, clean it up now. Am I getting through? I understand that nothing dies on the internet and once there, can always be found again one way or another, but you don't have to make it easy.

Whether it's fair or not, the reality is that employers all want young, fresh ideas coming in the door but they also want their employees to "look" like them. Once you get the job and prove how brilliant you are at it, *then* you can become the person you are meant to be - but not while you're trying to get your foot in the door for your first job out of school.

In one of my previous employment incarnations at a billion-dollar real estate corporation, I was recognized by my regional office as "the loose cannon". But, at one point, I had the highest profitability per square foot in my operation versus all other similar operations across the country. Over time, my immediate supervisor recognized that I was more likely to beg forgiveness after the fact rather than ask permission up front, but my deals spoke for themselves.

Remember the REALLY Useful Job Search Tactics mantra: If you are **making your company money or saving your company money**, you will be given more leeway (appearance, attitude, etc.) within corporate norms. Just not before you've proven yourself.

SEEKING STATEMENT

Immediately following your contact information, center and bold your Seeking Statement. Your Seeking Statement is non-negotiable; you must have one. You must tell your reader exactly what it is that you want. No one will read an entire resume and say, "Hey! Here's someone I need to hire!" No matter how successful you were in college, no matter your grade point average or your abundance of extracurricular activities, you are – sorry - just one of the equally talented thousands looking for a first job.

Don't let me sour your outlook. Anyone who knows you knows you are the best, but the recruiter and hiring manager *don't* know you. So you must make it as easy as possible to set yourself above the fray and the clutter.

Your Seeking Statement tells the employer exactly what you want. After that is clearly communicated, he will review the rest of your resume.

SAMPLE SEEKING STATEMENT

I am seeking an entry-level financial position at Giant Financial Inc.

That's it. One line that says it all. And there is nothing wrong – actually, everything right - about naming the company you want to work for in your seeking statement. (Just don't forget to change it for each resume you send.)

EDUCATION

In Chapters 1 through 4 (you've read those, right?), you learned about the REALLY Useful Job Search Tactics Superior Two Windows Resume format. For job seekers with experience, the next section of your resume focuses on accomplishments and then provides educational information at, or near, the end of the resume. But without significant professional experience, an entry-level job seeker should list educational accomplishments next – those that have been most recently achieved. It's a simple one-line statement with no embellishment:

PARK UNIVERSITY, BACHELOR OF SCIENCE MANAGEMENT, MAY 2006

You can enhance it with your grade point average (if it is exceptional) or mention any impressive, relevant information such as a double major or that you graduated with honors (cum laude, summa cum laude, etc.). But that's it. Save other details for the interview.

If you have just graduated from college, you may want to list other schools you have attended – other colleges, a junior college, even high school. But only if they enhance your resume by giving the recruiter or employer information that is pertinent to hiring you.

OBJECTIVE STATEMENT

Because you have no professional experience yet, your Objective Statement will set the tone of your resume and, possibly, your interviewing experience. This is your chance to tell your prospective employer how you will apply your education and training to **save him money or make him money.**

An Objective Statement will be short, clear and direct.

SAMPLE OBJECTIVE STATEMENT

My objective is to apply my education and on-the-job training I receive to contribute to the success of the company with the intention of increasing owner/shareholder value. I am willing to relocate across town or across the country to obtain the right position.

This statement may be excessive depending on your educational level, or personal style, but the point is to tell them you intend to *contribute* to the company. When others are asking all the wrong questions about vacation time and salary increases, you are sticking with the REALLY Useful Job Search Tactics mantra: **make them money/ save them money** and that will make any employer sit up and pay attention to *you*.

SELECTED ACCOMPLISHMENTS

Remember that scratch list of accomplishments I told you to make at the beginning of this chapter? Now is the time to pull it out so you can turn it into a statement that will show a recruiter or hiring manager that even without professional experience, you have the qualities needed to fit the job.

You need a total of between three and six achievements to list on your resume. These are talking points from which the interviewer will commonly begin the conversation. So choose them well, be prepared to expand on them and be proud. If you held any internships during school, these are a "must include" for your Selected Accomplishments list.

If you were an Uber-student involved in every sport, every committee and every volunteer activity who has won every award since age six, you'll need to pare down the number of accomplishments to the top six, maximum. Choose your best and be prepared to speak to how they have helped prepare you for life, your chosen career, or in what manner they will enhance your contribution to the workplace.

I know. You're thinking the only reason you took that job at Mickey D's was to have some spare cash to party or buy those perfect shoes or buy your own car. Probably true enough, but now let's write it resume-style in a manner that will impress an employer. Think back on that job with these powerful terms job-seeking terms in mind: Dedication, Dependability, Teamwork, Responsibility, Reliability, Growth, Loyalty. Sound phony? They aren't to an employer.

Here's a real-life example: I have a son who is now in the music business in New York City. When I was helping him build his resume, he was embarrassed to mention that from age 16 until he finished Recording/Business School, he had worked at a fabric and hobby shop. Not only was it the only job he had held all those years, it was – to a young man who wants to be in the music business – so, well, not cool.

But to an employer, this long-term job spoke of all those powerful terms above that you, as a job applicant, want to convey. Here is one of my son's Selected Accomplishments entries for that time period:

Employed from age 16 with the same company throughout high school and recording school beginning as a stocker and "retiring" as head cashier.

Do you see how the "responsibility", "dependability", "teamwork", "loyalty" and "reliability" pop out of that statement without having to directly name them? An employer will. And there is plenty of room for questions and discussion during the interview to expand on and "brag" about job responsibilities.

Now your job is to create such statements for each of your three to six personal best accomplishments.

WORK HISTORY/PERSONAL HISTORY

If you have a work history, a volunteer history or other special efforts you have contributed to your community, this is the place on your resume to list them. Just like any experienced professional would format their resume, list the most recent first and then go back in time. A review of Chapter 2 will give you more detailed instructions for this section.

If you don't have a work history, fill this space with whatever kept you busy while your friends were working their first jobs. This isn't a black mark on your life, but you do need to account for your time.

Give some thought to those power words we used for the

accomplishments section: loyalty, dependability, etc. If you played team sports, that's an easy fit. Creating a garage band, playing music and performances of any kind build the values embodied in those words. If you "only" volunteered or spent all your time with sororities or fraternities, you gained experience: you may have been a leader in these groups or organized new systems that improved how they operated. Indicate these things on your resume. And if you filled out just one college application, somewhere on it you supplied some of this same information. Dig it out and rework it to fit your current circumstances and your resume.

INTERVIEW POINTERS

There are many good books about how to ace job interviews and I won't repeat them here. But there are some REALLY Useful Job Search Tactics pointers you probably won't find in those books – and these are tactics that work.

Put Your Money Where Your Mouth Is

I told this story in the Introduction but it's worth repeating to any entry-level job seeker. This is a tactic (unplanned as it was) I used as a 19 year old applying for a job in a lumberyard as a helper/forklift driver. I told the interviewer, the vice president in charge of the yard, "for every dollar he paid me I would give him $10 back".

After the boss pulled his eyebrow down from the ceiling, he took a minute to look me over—all 125 pounds of me—and then tossed a pair of work gloves across the desk and told me to come back the next morning.

I had a good time and a successful run with that company. The idea I want you to take from this story is simple: the mantra I keep repeating – **make them money/save them money** – is crucial in convincing an employer to hire you - to give you a chance. This statement may be the only reason you get that chance!

Appearance and Presentation

Be yourself, be sincere, be respectful and dress professionally. It's okay to be nervous; you are not the first young person to show up in front of a hiring manager. Don't be afraid to speak to your passions and how, as a result, you are going to do a bang-up job. Brag about yourself to the point - you know how far to go - that you express profound confidence that you can do the job.

Ask For The Job

If you determine you want the job, *ask* for it. There is nothing wrong with saying, "I want this job...and I won't let you down."

Do Your Homework

Research the company before you go in for the interview. There is no excuse whatever for not knowing what the company does and where it is headed. You know how to search out this stuff online.

Prepare Your References

Ask former supervisors, friends of the family, clergy and any other important people you (or your parents) know to reference for you. The better their title, the better the reference. Be sure to tell your references that someone may call to inquire about you so they are not surprised when it happens.

Do not add these references to your resume. Keep a separate list of names, companies and titles with telephone numbers ready to supply a potential employer when they ask you for them. References placed on a resume do little more than to prove your inexperience and show a lack luster attempt to look "important" by name-dropping. Spend the time and use the space instead to show how perfect you really are for the position.

One Last Thing

Let the interviewer know that he or she won't be sorry they gave you a chance. And someone will do that. I promise.

☆☆☆☆☆☆

REALLY Useful Job Search Tactic #13:

DEVELOP YOUR ENTRY-LEVEL RESUME AROUND PERSONAL ACCOMPLISHMENTS AND ACHIEVEMENTS. FOCUS ON POWER WORDS SUCH AS "DEPENDABLE", "LOYAL", "TEAM PLAYER", "RESPONSIBLE".

REALLY Useful Job Search Tactic #14:

TELL THEM YOU ARE GOING TO MAKE THEM MONEY OR, BECAUSE OF YOUR ABILITY TO WORK HARD, YOU ARE GOING TO SAVE THEM MONEY.

REALLY Useful Job Search Tactic #15:

DON'T BE AFRAID TO ASK FOR THE JOB.

THE SUPERIOR Professional Mom's RESUME

"I've learned that every working mom is a superwoman."
- Uma Thurman

It should be different, but it's not. Stay-at-home moms – and dads too, these days (although they get more credit for being "cool"...why is that?) get no respect for the amazing job they do. Especially when it's time to re-enter the workforce. But whether you've been running your home for three or five or 10 or even 20 years, with some honest appraisal of the skills you've acquired and a sense of humor, you can overcome a challenging employment environment.

As I told the graduating students in the Entry-Level Resume chapter, if you have skipped forward to this chapter, go back now and read Chapters 1 through 4. They explain in detail the fundamentals of the REALLY Useful Job Search Tactics Superior Resume that you need to know before you can adapt them to your special circumstance.

One important item before we get started. Just in case you think you've "only" been keeping house and raising kids all these years, fire up your computer and type mom.salary.com into the address bar (you can also type in dad.salary.com) and run the Mom Salary Wizard (or Dad Salary Wizard) to see what all the professional jobs you do without a paycheck – such as daycare center teacher, facilities manager, computer operator, driver, CEO, cook, housekeeper, janitor, psychologist, etc. – are worth on the open market. Does $134,000 a year sound about right?

Now we're going to translate those expensive skills into a resume that will impress a potential employer. Doing this requires a sense of humor on your part, but that doesn't mean anything about this is funny. And if an employer doesn't get the point of your jest, it's my advice that you find a different potential employer. Yours is a special circumstance that takes a specialized approach.

Let's get started so you can see what I mean.

OBJECTIVE STATEMENT

As with all resumes, your name, in bold, goes at the top, followed by your contact information. Below that, centered, add your one-sentence Seeking Statement that tells recruiters and potential employers exactly the work you are looking for.

So far, this looks like every other kind of Superior Resume, as it should. Now, for your Objective Statement, instead of stating what you can accomplish for an employer, you tell them what you are *capable* of. It goes like this:

> **I am capable of supervising a small, intense group of subordinates while managing several unrelated projects focusing on the good of the overall organization.**

What you just described is management of a household with several children and the local Parent Teacher Organization, too. The only difference from the usual description, "stay-at-home-mom," is that you expressed it the language and manner of a business professional.

At interviews, you can be candid about why you believe it is an honest description of your ability to take your immediate past experience and apply it in a formal business setting.

If you are uncertain that such a statement is true, keep reading. In the next section you will see how accurate it is, and any recruiter or hiring manager who doesn't see it, doesn't deserve your talents.

ACCOMPLISHMENTS

In Chapters 2 and 3, you were asked to prepare a list of accomplishments and achievements. If you skipped that step because you thought a fulltime mom (or dad) doesn't have any that apply, do it now before you go any further. Thinking about your new Objective Statement will help you make – or add to – the list.

With that list in hand, select the best four to six accomplishments, the ones of which you are most proud and are the most "braggable." This is where the humor I mentioned above comes into play. Your top accomplishments, when written for your resume, should look something like this:

- Responsible for home-schooling three students who have all been accepted at major universities across the nation.

- Created and implemented a $2,000,000 marketing and advertising campaign resulting in net revenues of $16,000,000 for client and won a Best-In-Category national advertising award.

- Aggressively involved in the day-to-day operation of the Peterson Family Enterprise including the timely payment of all accounts receivable, inventory management, payroll, supervision of all Enterprise members, as well as directing family investment strategy.

Each accomplishment, stated in the language recruiters and hiring managers understand, plays to the REALLY Useful Job Search Tactics mantra, **save them money/make them money**. The first sample accomplishment above is of the utmost importance and regard. The second is from this professional mom's previous career. The third accomplishment is a humorous take on a group of skills that are too frequently dismissed, now presented somewhat tongue-in-cheek with a "let's take this seriously" attitude.

You should be proud of what you've accomplished. Maintaining a family, keeping them all well and healthy, managing the household and directing personal retirement or college funds is big business (just ask the guys you invest your retirement income with) and those skills are transferable to the marketplace.

You can also list such accomplishments as charitable and volunteer events and organizations you have been involved with or coordinated, sports projects and school activities. In the business world, people are paid real money for the stuff you've been doing as a matter of course. By translating your experience into business terms with a dash of (serious) humor, you can convince a recruiter or hiring manager that the skills you've developed as a professional mom are valuable and will contribute to the bottom line of the company.

EMPLOYMENT HISTORY

You can have just as much serious fun with your employment history. You know the format (because you read Chapters 2 and 3, right?), so let's jump right into how to turn professional mom-ism into successful Superior Resume style. Two examples:

Peterson Family Enterprise   1987 to present
    Chief Operating Officer & Co-CEO
The Peterson Family Enterprise represents the very best of what the Peterson Family has to offer to the community.

Community Newspaper Advertising   1980 - 1987
    Marketing & Advertising Manager
Community Newspaper represents the promotion and advertising interests of local newspapers in small towns across America with a specific focus on California papers.

Be prepared with some good accomplishment-focused stories to augment your COO position in the Peterson Family Enterprise. You might tell the interviewer that "the Enterprise continues to function on a solid fiscal basis. In fact, we are doing quite well, thank you, but the kids are growing up now and I am ready to return to the professional business world..."

I guarantee, with these light-hearted but business-focused descriptions of your work as in the Peterson Family Enterprise on you resume, you will have plenty of interview opportunities to expand on your accomplishments.

EDUCATION, AWARDS AND HONORS

Finish off your resume in the usual manner: education, honors and awards, keywords (and invisible keywords discussed in Chapter 4) that will help move you swiftly back into the workforce.

CONCLUSION

It's serious business finding a job, but that doesn't mean you can't have some fun doing it. Turning mother- or fatherhood on its ear and looking at it as a business enterprise not only highlights the real skills and accomplishments potential employers too often overlook, it does it with a sense of respect and a dash of humor.

If a recruiter or company manager doesn't appreciate that, find some other company that will. You've spent a long time at the most important job there is – raising the next generation. It's a whole lot more than PTO meetings, Barney and Harry Potter, so find an employer who knows that and appreciates you for what those years of your efforts at home can bring to his bottom line.

☆☆☆☆☆☆☆

REALLY Useful Job Search Tactic # 16:

THE KEY TO THE PROFESSIONAL MOM/DAD RESUME IS THE OBJECTIVE STATEMENT. TELL THE READER WHAT YOU ARE *CAPABLE OF DOING* FOR THEM

A DISCUSSION ON COVER LETTERS AND REFERENCES

"Be who you are and say what you feel,
because those who matter don't mind,
and those that mind, don't matter."
- Dr. Seuss

YOU'VE GOT IT ALL BACKWARDS

If you have spent even half as much time writing your cover letter as your resume, and if your paper cover letter is attached on top of your print resume, you've got it backwards. Here's what happens when a recruiter or hiring manager opens your envelope (assuming you mail it or hand it over in person):

- She immediately places your cover letter behind your resume

- She gives your resume a 5-to-30-second review

- IF your resume is of interest, she flips back to read the cover letter

Get it? Your Seeking Statement and your achievements and accomplishments on your resume are what the recruiter cares about first. The cover letter is a *supporting document* only and should be in secondary position behind your resume. Most importantly, it is not about you.

NOT ABOUT YOU?

Nope. A good cover letter exists to tell a potential employer that you understand the company's goals and you know how you can fit into their organization. There was a time when finding the kind of corporate information you need to make these statements was difficult. Today, you can learn a lot about a company's mission and future plans on its website, and what isn't explicitly stated can often be read between the lines.

With that information and the job description you are good to go to tell them why they should interview you. Remember, as I said earlier, the sole purpose of your resume is to get the interview where you will dazzle them with your knowledge and your ability to **make them money or save them money.**

THE SAME OLD LETTER

Everyone has written them in the past - the identical, "blanket" cover letter that goes out with every resume - the one that says you're a team player who can fit in anywhere; that you are—one m-o-r-e time - that dynamic individual...yada, yada, yada. Drop it. Delete it now. It won't help your job search and this letter can actually harm it.

When your cover letter shows no knowledge of the company or the job, the hiring manager or department chief knows you haven't bothered to learn anything about the organization and his or her response is "N-e-x-t!" as your resume lands in the trash.

THE SUPERIOR COVER LETTER

Your new cover letter must convey that you understand the requirements of the job itself, the overall mission of the company and how you are suited to fulfill those goals better than other candidates. And, it must be short. In no more than three or four sentences, you must:

- Prove your interest with some key points about the job and the company
- Present an overview of your qualifications in relation to the job
- Include a Call To Action

And, when possible, it should tell the reader how you will **make them money or save them money.**

The final sentence of your cover letter is always a **call to action**, a brief note asking for the job and, very importantly, asking the reader to *do something*. This is the easiest part of your letter and can be as simple as:

"I am ideally suited for this position and I look forward to speaking with you."

OR

"With two week's notice, I can begin work. Please call as soon as you are able."

Keep it brief and straightforward. Don't mess around with "I *hope* to hear from you soon". Remember, your focus is to be compelling and memorable.

✱✱✱

It's not a slam-dunk to write a good letter that covers all these bases and is short as well. Volumes have been written on the subject and there are many of them at your local bookshop. I recommend that you find one that suits your needs, particularly if you seek work in the medical, legal or engineering fields.

With a little practice and not forgetting to research target companies on their websites, you will get the hang of it.

SAMPLE "SNAIL-MAIL" COVER LETTER

Jerry Job Seeker

Date

Mr. or Ms. Chris Smith
Director of Procurement
**{If the name of the recipient is unknown, follow the lead in the
job listing such as Dear Recruiter, etc.}**
Human Resources
Company Name
Street
City/State/ZIP

Re: Reference #723 Buyer/Planner II (Insert *exact* job title as listed in
posting.)

{If the name is unknown}
Dear Recruiter (or Dear Hiring Manager:)

Having seen the Buyer/Planner posting on your corporate website,
I am submitting my resume for your consideration. My credentials
meet or exceed those required for this position.

I know that the Giant Corporation plays a significant role in supplying
the U.S. Army with specialized motor vehicles and my past experience
makes me uniquely capable of supporting and enhancing that goal.

If you seek a person who is up-to-date with current technology and
willing to go the extra mile to accomplish your mission, then I am the
right person for the job. I look forward to hearing from you soon.

Sincerely,

Jerry Job Seeker
Home: 123.456.7890   jerryjobseeker@emailaddress.com
Cell: 123.456.7891   www.&personalwebsite.net/jerryjob

EMAIL COVER LETTERS

In an email, your "cover letter", such as it is, is nothing more than a basic introduction and sincere thanks for someone taking the time to review your resume. That is all that needs to be said. Only a sentence or two.

When you submit your resume by email, you can omit the date, which will appear automatically in the email header. Your email address (though redundant), website address and telephone numbers should appear at the bottom of the cover letter following your name. Why repeat your email address? Your email may be printed or copied and pasted in such a way that your header will be cut off. So, just to be safe...

Also, omit the name and street address of the company, and begin your email cover letter with Dear Hiring Manager or Dear Mr./Ms. Smith.

PERSONAL REFERENCES

Never include references on your resume or in your cover letter. Unless specifically asked for, they are rarely needed until your application for a position has progressed beyond the first interview. But you should have them typed out neatly to provide when, and only when, you are asked for them.

Choose your references carefully. Uncle Ralphie and your best friend Regina may believe you are CEO material, but a recruiter or hiring manager, speaking with your Uncle and best friend, will quickly recognize they are not professional references and your credibility will plummet.

Your references should span your employment history – the most recent being best. Previous supervisors are always a best choice, people who can speak from the first-person about your responsibilities, achievements and work style. Three or four references are enough and the more senior their titles, the better. One personal reference is a good idea, although not a requirement, and if you are new to the job market or not too many years removed from college or recent classes upgrading your skills, a professor or teacher can be included.

In listing your references, make it as easy as possible for your prospective employer to contact them. Include name, company name, title, and telephone number but never an email address. Keep in mind that you will probably never provide a prepared reference list, as such, to a prospective employer. More than likely you will provide this information online or on a formal application. The sample page that follows is not intended as a handout—it is offered as a sample of what information you should always have on your person during your job search. It will come in handy.

IMPORTANT: Inform all your references that a potential employer may contact them about you. Be sure to get their permission to include telephone numbers—especially if you are providing an employer with a reference's home phone. And, while you're having that conversation, there is nothing wrong with coaching them to mention your positive achievements that could help secure the job for you, negatives ones they could minimize and any hot-button issues you gleaned from your interview that could have an impact.

REALLY Useful Job Search Tactic #17:

MAKE YOUR RESUME COVER LETTER ALL ABOUT THE COMPANY, THEIR GOALS AND MISSION, NOT ALL ABOUT YOU. THIS WAY, IT IS ALL ABOUT YOU.

REALLY Useful Job Search Tactic #18:

PROVIDE THE VERY BEST REFERENCES YOU CAN AND COACH YOUR REFERENCES ON THE HOT-BUTTON ISSUES THAT THEY CAN ANTICIPATE DISCUSSING WITH AN INQUIRING INTERVIEWER.

SAMPLE REFERENCES PAGE

Jerry Job Seeker References

Home: 123.456.7890   jerryjobseeker@emailaddress.com
Cell: 123.456.7891   www.&personalwebsite.net/jerryjob

Mr. Tory Evans   Immediate Supervisor, Director Acquisitions
Giant Sport & Entertainment Company
1234 Giant Street
Phoenix, AZ 88018
480.123.4567

Mr. Aric Adams   Family Friend
Vice President, A & R
Giant Music Company
2345 11th Ave
NY, NY 10001
212.123.4567

Mr. Stefan Carr   Personal Friend and Mentor
President/CEO
Giant Interactive Company
3456 Main St.
Houston, TX 77019
713.123.4567

Ms. Mary Elizabeth   Immediate Supervisor/Summer Internship
Attorney at Law
Giant Law Firm
4567 Jackson
Richmond, TX 77400
281.123.4567

Dr. R. Smeed, PhD   Economics Professor & Mentor
Professor
University of Anywhere
5678 University Square
Dallas, TX 77023
214.123.4567

THE MIGHTY, MIGHTY NETWORK

"It's not what you know, it's who you know!"
- Unknown

Here's some bad news for a family out there: someone just died. Here's the good news for someone else: a job just opened up.

Ooooh! Not a happy illustration. I know. But this is the real world and it happens everyday.

Somewhere else, just now - an employee got so angry, he walked off the job! And on the other side of town, a woman who was planning to return to work after maternity leave just changed her mind and decided to stay home and become a professional mom. Whatever the reason, one person's leaving a job creates an employment opportunity for another.

Thousands of jobs need filling every day because someone leaves - for whatever reason, but you won't know about any of these jobs from the usual sources. Statistics vary, but somewhere between 60 and 80 percent of all jobs are never listed in the newspaper or on job websites. Why? Because someone knew someone in the job market who was "perfect for the job" and they were offered the position in a very short period of time.

That is where the power of the mighty network comes in—and mighty it is! To have access to those unlisted jobs, you need to network relentlessly, so let's get started.

BRANDING AND MARKETING YOURSELF

In the context of REALLY Useful Job Search Tactics, the most important idea behind networking is marketing.

Have you ever heard of Target? Chevrolet? Microsoft? Of course you have. Every company whose brand name you instantly recognize achieved that recognition through marketing campaigns. And that's what you must do: become a recognizable brand by marketing yourself.

Although it will take some effort on your part, it's not hard to do. The trick is to be as effective at marketing yourself as possible without spending money or time unwisely.

✔ **Networking** is simply another way of saying, "branding." Companies large and small go to great lengths to brand themselves so you will think of them first. You must brand yourself so that everyone who can possibly be of any help will think of you first.

Your Three Personal Marketing Networks

There are three levels at which to market yourself. I will list them here and later in this chapter, I will explain how to effectively use each of them.

- **Immediate Network**

  Family, close friends, professional work circle

- **Secondary Network**

  Acquaintances you run into at the grocery store

  Kids' friends' parents you see at soccer practice, church groups, etc.

- **Expanded Network**

  The new network you will create; people you don't yet know

The first two networks are simple to access. It is the third that will take some work and will likely become the most important source in your job search. These are the people who will provide you with the best information in the job market.

Your goal, through networking, is to quickly find where there is a job opening that fits your skills or, even better, where one may soon be created, when it will happen, and how you can get the interview for it.

The people in your third network can often coach you – that is, give you important added information such as why an opening exists, what the corporate culture is and what level of skill or knowledge is required to do the job.

YOUR NETWORKING TOOLS

Networking Tool No. 1 - Job Seeking Business Card

This is the single most important marketing tool you have in your arsenal and it must be professional looking. Home-printed business cards are fine if you get the "clean edge" (vs. perforated) print stock. This is important because you want to present a polished look. Remember, for every one of "you" out their seeking a job, there are undoubtedly several hundred others with the same or similar skills. So you must have cards on your person that allow you to make contact quickly and professionally in order to be considered.

Your job-seeking business card can do that. It is a micro-resume that tells the reader who you are and what kind of job you are looking for. The front of the card includes:

- Your name
- Telephone number(s)
- Email address
- Website address, if you have one

- An abbreviated seeking statement

Keep it clean and simple. Notice in the following sample how little information there is, but how much it says.

FRONT OF JOB SEEKING BUSINESS CARD

> ### Jerry Job Seeker
> (123) 456-7890 Home
> (234) 567-8901 Cell
>
> jerryjobseeker@yahoo.com
> www.jerryjobseeker.com
>
> **Seeking a position in Sr. Level Hotel/Motel management**

The back of your business card will hold a micro-biography of who you are and what you will do for your future employer. As with your Superior Resume, you must show how you will **make them money or save them money.** This could be the reason you, and not someone else, gets the interview.

BACK OF JOB SEEKING BUSINESS CARD

> BS, University of Houston
> Conrad Hilton College of Hotel and
> Restaurant Management
> - 8 years managing 5-star waterfront property
> - 4 years managing internationally-recognized chain of 16 motels across southeastern U.S./ Recognized for achieving highest return on room rate for 3 consecutive years
> National Hotel/Restaurant Association award for Star Quality Industry Standards 3 years in a row

If you can afford it - and it's money well spent - have your business cards made at your local printer or you may choose to find an online business card printer which are often less expensive (or even free by providing you cards with their logo on back—meaning you will have to lose the back side copy) and will ship your cards within a week or so of you submitting your order over the internet.

Once you have your cards in hand, *never* leave the house without 30 or 40 them and never return home with any of them! Give a minimum of two to every person you run into so they will have one to keep and one to pass on to someone else. Hand them out in church, at your kids' soccer game, the gym and, you will need plenty of them for the networking groups I will tell you about in a moment. You never know who may call as a result of this effort.

Networking Tool No 2: The 30-Second Elevator Pitch

Imagine you're in an elevator and someone asks what you do. You have only a few seconds. What do you say? The person asking could be a hiring manager or may know of an opportunity right down the hall. That is the genesis of the name of this tool, but you need it in many other circumstances too. It requires that you state in no more than 30 seconds who you are, what kind of job you are seeking and how you can **save an employer money or make an employer money.**

That last item is the REALLY Useful Job Search Tactics approach and most people never include it in their 30-second pitch. But *you* will, because this is what will set you apart from the crowd of job seekers.

It doesn't sound difficult to talk about yourself for only 30 seconds, but it takes preparation and practice to make a powerful and compelling impression in so short a period of time - *and* to have the presence of mind to hand out your business card, too. But you can do it.

Think of what you wrote for the back of your business card and write out a script that you can memorize. Use words like "opportunity" rather than "job." Say, "will" rather than "would like to." These are small turns of phrase, but their impact can be substantial.

Here is what Jerry Job Seeker might say:

> "My name is Jerry Job Seeker and I'm an experienced professional in hotel and motel management. Most recently, I was general manager of a five-star property in Miami where over four years, I raised employee performance and created new streams of revenue. I'm looking for an opportunity to duplicate those efforts and earn a good income while doing it. Here's my card. I would appreciate any help you might be able to provide. May I have your card too?"

That's a powerful 30 seconds worth of information and it makes Jerry a compellingly interesting job seeker. Let's parse this speech and see what Jerry accomplished in 30 seconds:

- Jerry says who he is and what he does:

  My name is Jerry Job Seeker and I am an experienced professional in hotel and motel management.

- He then tells his elevator companion where he has been and what he *achieved* there:

  Most recently, I was general manager of a five-star property in Miami where over four years, I raised employee performance and created new streams of revenue.

- He follows that with a declaration of what he is currently seeking:

  I'm looking for an opportunity to duplicate those efforts and earn a good income while doing it.

- He offers his job seeking business card and asks for help:

  Here's my card. I would most appreciate any help you might be able to provide.

- And, lastly, he asks for his listener's business card:

  May I have your card too?

A big secret to a well-presented elevator pitch is to say your piece and then stop talking. I mean that. Don't say another word. Shut up. This is a common and time-honored sales technique and it is hard for some people to do. But you want the next person who speaks to be your listener. Even if he or she has nothing to offer at that time, you are allowing space and time for him to respond and giving him a measure of respect for the opportunity to make your pitch. That will make you memorable which, after all, is your goal.

Too many times I have seen a 30-second elevator pitch go on for a minute or more - and that will sink you. You may as well walk away from the moment.

So hone your speech and practice it. Pay attention to your vocal style. Show confidence. And be prepared - you never know when an opportunity will present itself and remember: luck is five percent opportunity and 95 percent preparation. Your practice time is that 95 percent.

Let's get back to your three personal networks and how to use them.

1. Immediate Personal Network

Your immediate network consists of those people who love you, care about you and want to see you succeed - your family, close friends and business colleagues. Not too many years ago, there was a stigma attached to having been laid off, downsized or fired, but no more. Everyone knows the nature of business and the new economy, so there is no need to be shy about your circumstances.

Tell everyone in your immediate network that you are seeking a job. Supply each one of them with a handful of your job seeking business cards to give to anyone they run across who may have an opportunity that will suit your skills. Most of all, remind them that they should acquire the name of any contact they find and that person's telephone number - minimum. Any other information is helpful (such as a business card), but you can get by with just the name and number.

2. Secondary Personal Network

Your secondary network consists of those people you see regularly or conduct business with, but don't really know - the guys at the hardware store, the people in the department store, grocery store and the coffee shop. They are excellent resources because they see people from different walks of life all day, every day and can pass on your business card. Chances are they already know people you would like to meet and they are already on a friendly basis with them.

Here's the point: the head of HR for Giant Company stops by the mechanic shop just like you. While she's waiting for an oil change, she's making small talk with the attendant who happens to mention - you. And then he hands over your job seeking business card. You have no way to know when this might happen, but it can't happen at all unless you initiate the process.

3. Expanded Personal Network

You don't know any of these people yet, but you soon will and they are the ones who will be most helpful in your job search. Some may even one day become your best friends. How will you find them? You will go out and look for them.

Attend local employment workshops, career fairs, seminars and state employment agency functions. Check your local newspaper and the internet for job networking opportunities. They are everywhere. Religious organizations conduct regular networking events that have a high degree of success.

There is no need to be shy about attending these events. Everyone there is or has been in your position, or is a professional who is there for the sole purpose of providing information and assistance to people looking for work. The camaraderie alone is fulfilling and you may be able to bring something to the table that will assist someone else in their search. Everyone gives at these events.

You will need to have with you four things for these meetings:

1. A bunch of your business cards
2. Several copies of your paper resume (that you will not offer unless asked)
3. A professional-looking notebook and pen
4. And in your head, your practiced and perfect 30-second elevator pitch

Hand out business cards to everyone you meet. You'll receive a lot of them too. Introduce yourself with your name and your seeking statement and nothing more—have your elevator pitch and your resume handy for anyone who asks for more information. Be prepared to casually inject in your elevator pitch how you have made money and/or saved money in the past for previous employers. In that notebook, record every bit of information you learn, as well as the leads you will acquire. All of this is great practice.

At networking events, you will come to appreciate the importance of brevity as you listen to 40 or 50 elevator pitches from other job seekers. Believe me, you will quickly learn to spot those who haven't prepared a pitch - they are the job seekers who *don't* notice that after about 30 seconds, *max*, nobody is paying attention! Don't be that person.

***

Invariably you will be told, on the spot, of opportunities that may fit you and your skills. And chances are good, in turn; that you will be able to pass on opportunities you have learned of in your job search. This is the beauty and power of networking - the interaction and exchange of valuable, just-in-time information. Step into a networking environment with a friendly, outgoing attitude and a willingness to help others and you will get a lot from the event - probably even a job.

Need I mention that any leads you acquire - from any of your three networks - require immediate follow-up? That's the next chapter: Working the telephone.

Networking Tool No. 3: Your Personal Email Address Book

The internet, has impacted how networking can be done. After you have created a powerful, compelling resume that you are proud of, go to your email account and open your personal email address book. Select the name of each person you have listed that could in any way, shape, or form possibly be of assistance in your job search. Your address book could possibly include contacts from all three levels of your personal networking effort. If you don't necessarily remember who a name belongs to or where you may know this person from (it happens all the time!) - send it! What have you got to lose? Take a moment to *briefly* explain your situation: "I am in the job hunt. Please forward my email to your address book." Ask everyone to keep their eyes and ears open for any opportunities they might hear of and, lastly, *tell* them what you are looking for—exactly! Don't expect anyone to know what it is you do!

Within the body of your email, make your contact information very easy to find. Lastly, absolutely, positively don't forget the most important component of your email: embed in the body of your email, *and* attach, a copy of your resume. Asking all those people to seek employment on your behalf without being able to forward a resume to their contacts is like asking a carpenter to build with no nails.

It is important you write this email as "generically" as possible while maintaining some of your personality. Why generic? Because you are going to ask *each person* who receives your email to forward it to *everyone* in their email address book who they think might be able to assist you in your search. I'm sure you understand the concept of multi-level marketing: 1 person sells to 3 people who sell to 3 people, and on and on and on.

Utilizing this formula, if only 3 people you send your resume to forward it on to only 3 additional people and this occurs 7 times your resume will have been disseminated to over 6500 people! This illustration is actually quite conservative when you consider that any one of our email address books probably contains tens if not hundreds of names!

Why not use this very same concept in your job search?! You have a vast wealth of contact, marketing, and networking information available at your fingertips. The potential exists that your REALLY Useful Job Search email will end up the in the inbox of several *thousand* individuals in a matter of days. And several of those individuals, whom you may never meet, received your email from a "friendly face".

You can reasonably expect to get some telephone calls with questions or leads quickly. Be prepared to come off in these calls like the professional that you are. This is a powerful REALLY Useful Job Search Tactic and the cost is right...nothing! Nada! Zip!

SAMPLE EMAIL NETWORKING TEMPLATE

Hi Everybody,

I am seeking employment as a _____ and would greatly appreciate your help.

Please take a moment to review my resume and forward it to anyone in your own email address book who you feel may be helpful to my job search or in need of my abilities.

Please call me ASAP if *you* know if any open positions I should pursue.

Thank You!

Name

Phone number(s)

Email address

A few hints of great importance here:

- First, if your email address is SlickChick@abc&d.com...change it. (You already know that one.)

- Second, be very certain that you project the professional "you" in the Subject Line that you place over your email. Say all that you can in a short phrase keeping in mind that this is the same subject line that will be re-sent, hopefully, over and over. Use something like: "Jerry Job Seeker/Professional Hotel Manager seeking employment opportunity".

- Third, begin your email with a seeking sentence clearly addressing what you are doing and why.

- Cross your fingers, say a little prayer, and hit "send".

As a matter of record, I have been presenting this little bit of free email networking advice for quite sometime now, and while I do not support or condone email spamming, this technique has met with a lot of success by individuals who have tried it. If you consider this tactic spamming (addressing those in your personal email address book), I respect your position on this matter but I go on record saying that my primary concern is first for any job seeking individual to obtain employment in any manner at their disposal as long as they do not lie or misrepresent themselves.

Networking Tool No. 4: Introducing Yourself Electronically

Let's face it; networking is the number one way in which all jobs are found. I also happen to know that networking is probably the number one most feared method for some people to expand their networks and let others know they are in the job hunt.

This is also an area where the internet has created a major and robust form of communication—the electronic networking site. Originally designed for business-to-business users to forge new connections on the "Six Degrees of Separation" concept, these sites have quickly and profoundly changed the way everyone can participate—at some level—in networking.

One of the most highly regarded methods of introducing yourself electronically for job seeking as well as conducting business in general is a website called LinkedIn.com. I have a profile registered on this site and I have no problem introducing people I know *personally*, to significant parties of interest from whom they may be able to seek employment connections. I am sure that there are, or soon will be, several other online services capable of providing this networking service.

Nevertheless, as much as possible, you still need to attend in-person events even if just to "practice" connecting to other people.

NETWORKING WARNING

Due to the constant and continuing threat of identity theft, regardless of what form of networking you may decide to pursue, never provide anyone with any personal information you know they don't need. *Social Security numbers are off limits no matter how good or important the reason may sound.* When it comes to employment, no one needs your Social Security number until they are ready to cut you a check or to conduct a background check (for which you must provide written authorization). I can also think of very few reasons anyone may need your physical address but that is one I leave up to you.

CONTINUE YOUR NETWORKING

Most people, as soon as they have their next job, stop looking for work and in an economy of outsourcing, downsizing and off shoring, that is a mistake. Remember, as I told you earlier, you are nothing but a line item in this year's budget - and it might be removed next year due to circumstances beyond your control. Always keep in mind that your time and position with any employer is ripe for budget cutting.

The average time spent on a job, any job these days, is only two-and-a-half to three years, so keep on networking even when you're working. The best time to find a job is when you don't need one.

REALLY Useful Job Search Tactic #19:

INFORM VIRTUALLY EVERYONE YOU KNOW THAT YOU ARE IN THE JOB MARKET. THE MORE YOU DO SO, THE MORE COMFORTABLE IT WILL BECOME.

REALLY Useful Job Search Tactic #20:

YOU MUST HAVE PERSONAL JOB SEARCH BUSINESS CARDS ON YOUR PERSON AT ALL TIMES. MAKE IT EASY FOR PEOPLE TO REMEMBER WHAT JOB YOU ARE SEEKING AND HOW TO CONTACT YOU.

REALLY Useful Job Search Tactic #21:

HAVE YOUR 30-SECOND ELEVATOR PITCH PERFECTED AND READY TO PRESENT AT THE DROP OF A HAT.

REALLY Useful Job Search Tactic #22:

CREATE A PERSONAL EMAIL AND SEND IT TO YOUR ENTIRE EMAIL ADDRESS BOOK INFORMING THEM THAT YOU ARE IN THE JOB HUNT. ASK EVERYONE TO FORWARD YOUR EMAIL ON TO EVERYONE IN HIS OR HER BOOK, AND ON, AND ON, ETC., ETC.

REALLY Useful Job Search Tactic #23:

SEARCH OUT AND INVESTIGATE THE POSSIBILITIES OF UTILIZING THE ELECTRONIC NETWORKING OFFERINGS FROM SITES SUCH AS LINKEDIN.COM

WORKING THE TELEPHONE

"What would you attempt to do if you knew you would not fail?"
- Dr. Robert Schuller

In some ways the internet has made the job search easy but at the same time, it has also made it more difficult. An oxymoron? Not really. In posting resumes and responding to job listings, too many people have an artificial sense of having done something significant in their search for employment. Because there are hundreds of thousands of resumes online, relatively few will be actually be seen by recruiters who also have hundreds of resumes emailed to them for each job they post.

Sooner or later, you must pick up the telephone.

For a few people, "working" the phone is a yes or no proposition. To those for whom cold calling is an adventure you relish, you probably don't need this chapter, but you might want to skim through it anyway. For those who go ashen and mute at the prospect of speaking to a stranger about a job, this chapter probably won't help, although it is still worth a read. But most of you fall somewhere in the middle who have realized that blasting your resume hasn't worked and waiting for the staffing agency to call isn't paying the bills. This chapter is for you.

You are ready to take charge of your job search and I'm sure you've figured out by now that the only way to move forward is to make personal contact with the one person who can make a difference - the hiring manager. It's a harsh, but true fact of job-search life that you must make the first contact and you will most likely have to do it by telephone.

In this chapter, I'll show you proven techniques of doing that along with some REALLY Useful Job Search Tactics tips and tricks.

THE GOALS

It can be daunting, call after call, but sooner or later you *will* connect with the person you are trying to reach and when you do, you need to be prepared to accomplish your goals. First, let's identify those goals. You want to get as many of the following as possible:

- The name and correct title of the hiring manager
- The hiring manager's business email address
- A direct phone number for the hiring manager
- Permission to call again in the future
- Permission to email your resume now

Remember, this is not the Human Resources department. You are calling the hiring manager of the department for which you want to work, and these are not out-of-line requests.

The best way to accomplish this goal is to create a script that will get you through the circumstances for each of the two people you are likely to reach on the telephone. In each instance, you are aiming to create a dialogue - a two-way conversation that will lead to the results listed above. Your script will contain:

Gatekeeper: Greeting

Gatekeeper: Reason for call

Hiring manager: Greeting

Hiring manager: Reason for call

Hiring manager: Call to action

I'm going to provide you some sample scripts for each situation. Use these as templates to write your own scripts. When they are written, practice with a friend and rewrite them until the scripts feel natural and you are pleased with your message. Keep your points short and most importantly in preparing your script: *never ask a question that can be answered with a yes or no.*

Every television interviewer and every sales person knows this rule in their bones. Such questions are conversation stoppers and they provide the person you're speaking with an opportunity to hang up. Instead, create a dialogue and you will be heard.

THE GATEKEEPER SCRIPT

Sometimes they are called receptionists or administrative assistants, but they are gatekeepers and their job is keep the gate closed to outsiders; to people the hiring manager doesn't know and doesn't want to speak with. Gatekeepers are trained to be fast, efficient and may have several calls on hold at once. Few mean to be brusque, but they will come off that way and you must deal with it. Don't take setbacks personally.

That said I believe most people are inherently friendly and willing to help. Helping others makes people feel good about themselves and when you are polite and clear about what you are asking for, they will usually do their best to help you.

When you prepare your script for the gatekeeper, include "Hello", "Goodbye" and everything in between. Your script is a work in progress, to be rewritten as you discover through successive calls what works best.

TACTIC NO. 1 – JUST ASK

Immediate Goal: To get the name of the person you want to speak with and get the opportunity to speak with him or her.

SCRIPT: *Hi, my name is Jerry Job Seeker and I could use your help. May I have the name of the vice president of manufacturing?*

You can expect the response to be: May I ask what this is in regard to?

> SCRIPT: *Yes, I am a manufacturing engineer. I'm new to the area and I'm looking for employment opportunities. I would like to introduce myself to the "boss," put a personal business card in the mail to see if he or she knows of any opportunities either with your company or others in the area.*

It doesn't matter if you are not new to the area. What matters is that you are a manufacturing engineer and "new to the area" often makes people more willing to help.If you are very lucky, the gatekeeper will give you the name of the VP and connect you. If not, you must get his or her name. Even if the gatekeeper says the person is unavailable, you still want to *"send a business card over with a note."*

Notice that you did not say, "resume." That word gets you transferred immediately to a pre-recorded job line or to the Human Resources gatekeeper. Not where you want to be. Keep in mind that if you get only a name, you are already ahead of at least 50 percent of other job seekers.

TACTIC NO. 2 – "JUST WANT TO PUT A CARD IN THE MAIL"

Immediate Goal: To get the name of the person you want to contact.

> SCRIPT: *Hi, my name is Jerry Job Seeker. I need your help. Can you give me the name of the VP of manufacturing?*
>
> GATEKEEPER: May I ask what this is in regard to?
>
> SCRIPT: *Yes, I represent a line of (fill in a product appropriate to the company) and want to put a brochure and my business card in the mail to him. May I have his or her name and your physical mailing address?*

You aren't representing anything and you won't be required to explain this fib to anyone later. The reason for this tactic is that you *must* get the name of your contact person. Once you have that, you are on easy street. You can call back later in the day and ask for that person by name or, if you are concerned about being recognized, wait a day.

Sales people use this tactic all the time to get the names of individuals they want to pitch. Anyone who calls a company and asks, with confidence, for the correct name of the individual he or she wants to speak with, will get that person on the line almost every time.

If you have any qualms about these techniques, remember that we are discussing REALLY Useful Job Search Tactics. You need to do whatever you reasonably can to get recognized and be considered for every potential opening that is available. These are not unreasonable job search tactics.

THE PUBLIC LIBRARY OPTION TO GETTING THE RIGHT PERSON'S NAME

If you haven't been to your public library lately maybe it's time. Your local library most likely has a Business Resource category in their online catalogs. This resource service may include some of the finest business databases that are only available to the public by subscription. Because your taxes already pay your subscription, all you have to do is obtain a current library card to gain access to these databases.

What's so great about access? These databases often have the names of C-Level company leaders (CEO, COO, CFO, etc.) as well as the names of senior executives and contact information. In short, a wealth of information is available to you at your library (and you thought it was just a place with a bunch of books!). Call or drop in and ask about business-to-business website access. I did and was astonished at the number and quality of business databases I now have free access to.

You Got The Boss On the Line! Now What?

First, breathe. You did well. You have the object of your quest on the telephone. Now is the time to focus on your script and remain calm. It may help to remember that he or she is a person like you who has family and considerations in life just like yours. Everyone is busy, but having gotten through to a vice president or hiring manager, you may not be treated in as short a manner as the gatekeeper may have treated you. This person has taken your call and when you begin to "talk the talk" - your industry or business lingo - your listener will know where you come from and that you two have something in common.

HIRING MANAGER: Hi, this is Steve.

SCRIPT (Use the name the Hiring Manager just used. If no name is given, address your listener as Mr. or Ms.): *Hi, Steve. This is Jerry Job Seeker. I'm a manufacturing engineer searching for employment opportunities. I was recognized in my last position for the amount of money I was able to save my company by going digital on the manufacturing floor. I'm calling to see if you would know of any openings that may be available in your office or in the area.*

Speak your piece and then listen. With the use of the **save you money** sentence, this is a powerful introductory statement and I can assure you, you have just created a dialogue. (Note: You are always looking for "employment opportunities", *never* a "job".)

If Steve knows of no openings or has nothing of real value to offer, immediately move on to a discussion asking about any local trade association luncheons or meetings where you might be able to network. But don't forget that your primary goal at this very minute is to get your resume into his hand. If no request for it is forthcoming from Steve, before you hang up ask permission to forward your resume so that Steve can keep it on hand *"in the event something comes along"* that he may not be aware of right now. This is what networking is all about.

SCRIPT: *Steve, thank you very much for your time. I sincerely appreciate it. May I get your email address and forward my resume over to you in case you should hear of something?*

(If Steve says "No", don't worry about it. Move on to your next "target". There is no networking to be done here—period.)

And your last question before closing:

SCRIPT: *Steve, if I don't find something before then, would you mind if I give you a call in a couple of months to follow up with you?*

You will almost always get a "yes" in answer to this question because no one expects you will really follow up.

Keep a log of all calls that includes the date, the name of the person you spoke with, telephone number, email address, what was said and anything memorable about the dialogue (e.g. son just broke his arm) that you can bring up during a follow-up call. Establish a **suspense date** - the date you plan to call again and then, if you are still in the job market, *do it.*

People are regularly blown away when someone actually does call back because so few do. In your follow-up call, tell the gatekeeper that you spoke to Steve near the end of July and he said it would be okay if you called back.

One Successful Call is Your Personal Icebreaker

It's amazing how many people who are fearful of making cold calls realize that it's not so difficult after all once they get one under their belt. The best time to make another cold call is right away, as soon as you hang up from the first. After you have a couple of trials behind you, you will be able to keep doing it. These are standard techniques for cold calling that sales people have been using successfully for years.

Personal Telephone TECHNIQUES

Your objective in working the telephone is to get an interview. If the best you can do in the beginning is one call a day, that's fine. Next, up your goal to one in the morning and one in the afternoon. And move on to more from there. I do understand how hard it is. Years ago, as a young puppy in the sales world, I had to learn too. Here are three tricks that will help bolster your confidence in any telephone situation:

1. Smile. This is an ancient radio announcer standby I learned from an on-air DJ friend. If you want to sound happy and confident on the radio, you must smile. Use the same technique for making (and taking) phone calls. Your smile and enthusiasm will come across the phone without effort and the difference it can make will astound you.

2. Stand. And move around a little bit if you can. Be expressive when you speak. It will keep you from slumping in your chair, which can reduce the confidence in your voice. Speak to your strengths and (you know this well by now) how you will **save them money or make them money.**

3. No background noise. Turn off any music. Move away from your computer. (One significant exception may be viewing the company site as reference during a call. In this case you need to be fairly familiar with the navigation of the site.) Turn off the ringers on any other telephones. It's also a good idea to turn off call waiting while you are telephoning; the little "hiccup" that happens when another call comes in always disrupts the dialogue. Focus on what you want to achieve. You will do it best when you are not distracted.

* * *

I started this chapter by acknowledging how difficult it is for some people to pick up the telephone and speak with a stranger about a job. I hope this may have eased your fears and that you will give it a try. I promise it will speed your job search. Either way, the next chapter, on the many ways the internet can aid your search, is stuff anyone can do without fear.

☆☆☆☆☆☆

REALLY Useful Job Search Tactic #24:

WORK THE PHONES. PREPARE A SCRIPT TO BEGIN A DIALOGUE WITH THE GATEKEEPER AS WELL AS THE PERSON YOU WANT TO CONTACT. DO NOT ASK QUESTIONS THAT CAN BE ANSWERED

WITH A YES OR A NO. DO POINT OUT THAT YOU WILL MAKE THEM MONEY OR SAVE THEM MONEY.

REALLY Useful Job Search Tactic #25:

CALL YOUR PUBLIC LIBRARY AND ASK IF THEY PROVIDE ACCESS TO SUBSCRIPTION-BASED BUSINESS-TO-BUSINESS (B2B) WEBSITES. IF THEY DO, FIND OUT WHAT YOU MUST DO IN ORDER TO GAIN FREE ACCESS.

THE INTERNET AND YOUR JOB SEARCH

*"The voyage of discovery is not in looking for new
landscapes, but in looking with new eyes."*
- Anonymous

The rules for job searching changed when the internet came to town. Now there is a cornucopia of tools and useful information that before, either didn't exist or were hard to find - company backgrounders, salary comparators, industry trends and job listings in every hill and dale in the country, even the world.

Networking is still the foremost way most jobs are found, but the internet is now the number two source and growing at an exorbitant rate. Used wisely, it is a spectacularly good source of both information and job listings. Whether you are seeking full-time work in the private sector, with the government - local or federal - a temporary job or freelance employment, the internet is your ally.

At the end of this chapter are important tips on making the best use of the internet for your job search but first, here are the kinds of employment sites you will find on the web.

The National Job Boards

You probably already know the names of the super-sized job boards:

Monster.com, CareerBuilder.com and Yahoo's HotJobs.com. These are unparalleled national employment websites that offer easy-to-use tools with vast numbers of available positions listed. And, because competition among them is fierce, they regularly add new features to make your search (and your life!) more productive.

Each of these websites wants you believe that theirs is the only one you need. Forget that. You owe no job board (or agency or company, for that matter) loyalty during your job search. Use them all. To badly paraphrase the Three Musketeers: "It's one for you and all for you."

On these job boards, you can post your resume, search listings by location, company, job title, industry and even, if you are thinking of relocating, find cost-of-living information, housing prices, mortgage brokers and moving companies for just about any community in the country.

Most convenient of all, you can set up a **search agent** that will deliver the latest job listings to your email inbox based on the keywords you have entered into their system. (If you are not certain how to use keywords, go back to Chapter 4, THE SUPERIOR Electronic RESUME, for a refresher.)

Here's how it works: if you are searching for a sales job, the words *sales, marketing, advertising* are good keywords to choose. Once you have set up that search – which on the national boards will also include location, industry and job title - every listing that matches one or more of those keywords and your other criteria will be forwarded to you with a link directly to each posting listed in the email. From there, you can follow the company or recruiter instructions for applying for the jobs that suit your search.

It's fast, easy and saves you enormous amounts of time reviewing listings on individual websites. And I have to say, if you are not using search agents and spending three hours or more a day online job searching versus an hour or so responding to email agents, you are fooling yourself if you think you are making quality progress.

Local Job Boards

I "cut my teeth" in the employment business beginning in 1997, by representing the first local employment website in the greater Houston area and by virtue of being first, we were far and away the most successful. I have seen first hand how beneficial and powerful a robust local website can be to the local job seeker.

The obvious benefit to using a local job site is that most all the available positions are in your "neighborhood." REALLY Useful Job Search Tactics is a fan of national job boards where there are a large number of diverse listings from every corner of the country—and beyond. But when it comes to finding a job locally, it does a local employer little good to post that position on a national site from which he is likely to get an unnerving number of resumes from job seekers who, even if qualified, can't relocate without financial assistance from the local employer. So you can anticipate finding jobs on local websites that won't be listed on the giants.

Like the national job boards, local employment websites will usually supply a **search agent**, although some do not. This tool is so useful and such a time-saver it should be the first feature you look for on any board and move on if it's not there.

A good local site will also list career fairs, networking groups and other information focused on the community it serves.

A word of caution: no reputable job board - national or local - charges you, the job seeker, for posting your resume or searching job postings. They make their money from employers who list jobs with them. Using job boards and responding to listings should never cost you a dime.

You may, however, encounter such services as resume writing, resume blasters (who, for a fee, will send your resume to "1000's of recruiters"), personal background checks and more. Try to determine their value to you and if you feel good about the service offered, go for it.

Corporate Employment Websites

If you know the company, or companies, you want to work for, visit their corporate website first. Every company of any value, large or small, has an employment section on its site listing job openings with at least an email address and/or fax number and sometimes an online application form with instructions on how to apply.

Additionally, you can learn a lot about the company and its philosophy on its website. It should always be your first stop in seeking information about the company background, philosophy, mission and method of operation. You'll be expected to know all this when you interview, so don't commit job-seeking suicide. With the internet, you have no excuse.

NICHE WEBSITES

Niche job boards cater to specific kinds of jobs and industries. Are you a manufacturing engineer? Search for the term and sure enough - there's a website named manufacturingengineer.com where you can post your resume and search listings. Perhaps you're Asian looking for a way to use your language skills. What do you think? asianjobs.com? You bet! It's there.

Check out trade organization websites and unions too. They have job listings, resume postings and a wealth of information about your employment niche.

Contract and Freelance Employment Job Sites

As companies move to hiring more contract and freelance employees, an explosion of sites targeting this kind of work are appearing. These are, in the purest sense, matchmaking services - not dating, but business matchmaking.

Let me give you an example. Many smaller companies may not be able to afford to keep a professional sales trainer on staff but require the services of such a person once or twice a year. This company can go to a contract or freelance employment site and post their need with dates and rate of pay. You, then, as an experienced sales trainer, can view their posting and offer and negotiate for your services by using the website's bid procedure.

These jobs can last from a few days to several years and some assignments have been known to send contractors/freelancers all around the globe.

There are many such sites you can find by searching "freelance employment" or "contract employment." Elance.com is one of the better sites I am familiar with that lists assignments both here, in the U.S., and abroad.

GOVERNMENT EMPLOYMENT WEBSITES

If you are seeking employment with any federal agency or significant government contractor, check out AmericasJobBank.com. (But you better hurry. The word as of this writing is that the government has decided to discontinue funding AJB.com sometime in 2007.) This is a comprehensive site with thousands of job listings that includes resume posting and a search agent to deliver new listings to your inbox.

In addition, every state has its own employment website which not only lists positions available within the government, but usually links to other major sites throughout the state that also serve job seekers.

City and county sites as well as independent school districts all have employment sections on their websites that list current employment opportunities.

Important Tips on Using Internet Job Boards

Resume expiration date: Almost all job boards will keep your resume in their database for only a specific period of time before deleting it (although some will keep old, out-of-date resumes in their archives forever just to make inflated resume-database claims). Some job boards may remove your resume after a year and some as soon as three to six months. It is important to note the term on each job board, set a reminder in your calendar and resubmit your resume on the expiration date. Most sites, however, with any type of update performed during the original posting, will reset the expiration date to day one making it appear on the site as new.

"Stale" resumes: Recruiters want to work with the freshest resumes and will notice a job seeker's posting date. Many will not look at resumes that are older than 90 days and some won't view resumes older than 30 days! Therefore, it is important to keep your resume as fresh-looking as possible by resubmitting it to the job board or "updating" it so that it appears near the top of the resumes recruiters are searching. You may want to "refresh" your resume as often as once a week. Often you can do so by opening your resume, retyping your name or resume title and hitting Submit. Your resume will appear to have "just landed new" on the site and will post at the top.

Active pursuit of jobs: Many recruiters post jobs on employment boards and *never* visit the resume database. And why would they? Within a couple of days of posting a position, they may receive from 200 to 2,000 responses. So it is imperative that you immediately pursue jobs that are sent to you via your pre-established **search agent**. Don't wait a day or two. They won't wait for you.

As convenient as employment websites make job seeking, remember that you cannot rely on them exclusively. To land the job you're looking for, you must simultaneously be networking, cold calling and using all the other REALLY Useful Job Search Tactics in this book.

☆☆☆☆☆☆

REALLY Useful Job Search Tactic #26:

SET UP A PERSONAL SEARCH AGENT ON EVERY EMPLOYMENT WEBSITE YOU VISIT SO THEY ARE ALL WORKING ON YOUR BEHALF 24/7.

REALLY Useful Job Search Tactic #27:

USE JOB BOARDS WISELY. DO NOT ALLOW THEM TO TAKE UP ALL YOUR TIME. YOU STILL NEED TO BE NETWORKING AND WORKING THE PHONES.

The Mature Job Seeker

"If you take all the experience and judgment of people over 50 out of the world, there wouldn't be enough left to run it"!
- Henry Ford

If you are a mature job seeker - that is, for our purposes, as young as 40 - you have probably already heard that annoying excuse for not being hired: You're overqualified. This is code, well known in the recruiting industry and beyond, for "you're too old".

Although it is commonplace, age discrimination in the workplace is illegal. Nevertheless, it is difficult to prove on the job and virtually impossible to prove in the job search. So what's an older job seeker to do?

One tactic is to do everything in your power to interview first not with the human resources department, but the hiring manager or department supervisor directly. He or she is more likely to be closer to your age (or simply appreciate your experience), which will help, but equally important, they will speak the language of your specialty. Your **Save Them Money/Make Them Money** statements will have more resonance with the person who has responsibility for the budget and that will reflect more positively on your experience and your age.

You can't help your age, but whether you interview with the manager or human resources, there are steps you can take to moderate its effect on young recruiters and hiring managers. And by the way, many of these measures apply equally to job seekers younger than 40. They are a good reminder for everyone.

APPEARANCE

First impressions matter. Being neat, clean and up-to-date shows your respect for the employer and the interviewer. I'm not talking about the latest fashion necessarily, but be sure your "interview outfit" is newly pressed, age-appropriate and fits well. Unless you're applying to be a fitness instructor, sneakers are not acceptable, so be sure your shoes are polished and the heels aren't rundown.

Believe it or not, extremist employment counselors have been known to suggest cosmetic surgery for older job seekers. I find that objectionable. But if coloring your gray hair shaves a few years off your appearance or gives you more confidence, you may want to consider it. Young recruiters will sometimes automatically dismiss applicants who look like their parents or grandparents.

ATTITUDE

"First line" recruiters tend to be young, so if your first interview is within the human resources department of a company, you will likely meet with a 20- or 30-something. You must pass this "audition" to reach the next level where you can speak with a department manager who is likely more familiar with the kind of work you do.

Unfortunately, too often it is up to you, the candidate, to "handle" the young interviewer who may be less comfortable with someone old enough to be his or her parent. These Do's and Don'ts will ease your path.

MATURE SEEKER DO'S

Be confident but not smug or condescending. Listen well, and treat your young interviewer with the same respect you would give someone your own age.

Answer quickly in the affirmative if you are asked if you can work with a supervisor who may be younger than you. If you're not comfortable in that situation, get over it before the interview. It is often the way of the work world these days.

Express your willingness to change your work habits when required and be prepared to offer examples of new skills you have acquired to keep up with the changing work environment.

Show passion for your skill, your experience and the value you can add to the company's bottom line. **Save you money/Make you money** applies as equally to older job seekers as young ones.

As I've mentioned in previous chapters, do your homework - know the company, its mission and objectives. Express how you have put sound thought into how you are going to become a vital and contributing member of their team.

Listen. Be professional and treat your interviewer, regardless of their age, with the respect and professionalism they deserve. You have to believe that there is a good reason that young person has earned the position they hold. Just maybe she has something on the ball. *And I would suggest you remember back to how important, mature, and valuable you were trying to be at 25, 35, and up!*

MATURE JOB SEEKER DON'TS

Don't be a know-it-all. (You don't.) Temper any inclination to prove that you've been there and done that long before the interviewer was born. Don't use such phrases as "in my day" or "that's not the way we used to do it" or conversely, "that's how I've always done it." Your way may still be the best, but then again, maybe it's not. Show your willingness to accept new ideas and suggestions.

Don't show irritation if the discussion turns to age. Contrary to common belief, it is not illegal to ask how old you are (See Note Below); it is only illegal to not hire you based on your age. The distinction is a legalism, for sure, but it is not necessarily prejudicial, so go with the flow, treat it with some humor and move onto your mantra: **Make them money or save them money.**

NOTE ON PRE-EMPLOYMENT INQUIRIES

"The ADEA (Age Discrimination Employment Act of 1967) does not specifically prohibit an employer from asking an applicant's age or date of birth. However, because such inquiries may deter older workers from applying for employment or may otherwise indicate possible intent to discriminate based on age, requests for age information will be closely scrutinized to make sure that the inquiry was made for a lawful purpose, rather than for a purpose prohibited by the ADEA."

Source: http://www.eeoc.gov/facts/age.html

Back in Chapter 3, I told you to omit non-essential dates such as high school and college graduation years and dates of previous employment. That is to ensure that your resume is not automatically dismissed during the initial review. Keep in mind, now that you have achieved the first interview, that the topic of age is not necessarily prejudicial and can usually be dealt with successfully if you remember the above Do's and Don'ts.

WHEN AGE DISCRIMINATION IS APPARENT

Just the same, sooner or later, most job seekers over 40 run into an interview situation in which he or she suspects - often correctly - that their age will disqualify them from consideration. The recruiter is superficially polite and usually careful not to cross the line into illegality, but may rush through the interview or not engage in a serious conversation. (You may want to take notes as the interview progresses. Taking notes in any job interview is completely acceptable.)

I call this instant the "moment the window drops". You can still see what is on the other side but you know that "something" has come between you and your interviewer and you know you haven't a chance of being hired because of your age. This instant is very apparent to a mature job seeker.

As I mentioned above, failure to hire for reasons of age is illegal, but lawsuits are almost never successful, and unless you have unlimited funds, are not good for your bank account. But here are some "Hail Mary" options that may or may not save the interview.

1. THE NO NONSENSE OPTION

The prohibition against racism and sexism in hiring is so strongly established in our culture now that no recruiter would dare openly voice such issues. Awareness of ageism is growing, but slowly, and it has not reached everyone's consciousness yet. Should an interviewer ever state or imply that you are too old for the position, immediately terminate the interview and ask to speak to the recruiter's supervisor.

Be polite with the supervisor, but firm. State exactly what the interviewer said to you and ask how the supervisor will resolve this illegal act. How far you determine to move on this matter is solely up to you and you may still not be hired, but you will have put the company on notice and probably instilled the fear of God (or at least, the government) in them. And it may help future mature job seekers.

2. THE BRAIN DRAIN ARGUMENT

In 2006, the oldest baby boomers began turning 60. Millions of them will retire when they become eligible for early retirement benefits from Social Security. There are 78 million boomers and only 56 million in the generation coming up behind to replace them in the workforce, yet the majority of corporations have been slow to address the "brain drain" problem they face. You can use this fact to your advantage in an interview.

If you have been told you are overqualified or suspect from other comments that your age is working against you, bring up the brain drain issue. If you've gotten to the point in the interview of considering this approach, you probably don't have anything to lose.

You don't need to be combative; it won't help anyway. But you can point out that you simply know more "stuff" than younger workers, are more experienced and have already learned from past mistakes you won't be making again.

If you can *professionally* and persuasively make this pitch, you may earn yourself the opportunity to take your interview to the next level: the hiring or department manager. And by making this argument, you might create a new path for those who follow you into the company.

3. THE "THE 4 QUESTIONS" OPTION

My friend, Ronni Bennett, who authors TimeGoesBy.net, a contemporary blog devoted to issues of aging as a positive experience, devised the following four questions to use when you know all chance of getting the job is gone and it's all about your age. Look your interviewer straight in the eye, don't blink and in your most pleasant, professional voice, ask:

- Does this company maintain a mixed-age workplace?

- How do you weigh the skills of younger and older workers in deciding whom to hire?

- How do you train young managers in dealing with subordinates who are old enough to be their parents and grandparents?

- Is my age an impediment to being hired at this company?

Ask these questions, and without any doubt, you have clearly and succinctly stated your case with no animosity but with uncommon capacity. You and I both know your interviewer has probably never been confronted so directly with such powerful questions.

These questions have the effect of bringing your age out as a topic of discussion along with your knowledge of the desirability for diversity in the workplace. If the answers are not suitably positive, you may want to rethink the idea of working there. At the very least, you'll feel good about challenging what you perceive to be age discrimination. And hey, there is always a chance the hiring manager, watching you in action, might just say we need your kind of no-nonsense person around here. You never know.

***

In the end, the goal is to be hired and these options may help. Age discrimination is, unfortunately, a fact of life, but there are many companies who do select new employees on the basis of skill and experience without regard to age, and as the brain drain dawns on employers during the next few years, more of them will, by sheer necessity, be hiring people well into their 60s, 70s and maybe beyond.

☆☆☆☆☆☆

REALLY Useful Job Search Tactic #28:

IF AT ALL POSSIBLE, INTERVIEW WITH THE HIRING MANAGER. LET THAT PERSON THEN INTRODUCE YOU TO HUMAN RESOURCES TO GET THE PAPERWORK DONE.

REALLY Useful Job Search Tactic #29:

FOLLOW THE DO'S AND DON'TS FOR MATURE JOB SEEKERS AND IF YOUR INTERVIEWER IS ON THE "UPHILL" SIDE OF 40, BE KIND. EDUCATE THE "KID" AND ENLIGHTEN HIM OR HER AS TO WHY YOU SHOULD BE HIRED. IF THAT DOESN'T WORK, SOCK 'EM WITH THE "4 QUESTIONS"!

THE INTERVIEW & YOUR SUPERIOR THANK YOU NOTE

"Diamonds are nothing more than chunks of coal that stuck to their jobs."
- Malcolm Forbes

When the telephone rings at the expected time, you know it's a preliminary telephone interview for a job. You know this because the recruiter responded to your excellent REALLY Useful Job Search Tactics Superior Resume and sent you an email requesting this pre-interview.

And you're ready for it because you've done your research. You've read the company website. You've Googled the company name to track down news stories about their products, services and people. You've read the online commentary – pro and con.

The recruiter on the other end of the phone has your resume, the one where you listed your Selected Achievements which leaves you a lot of room to talk about how you can serve the company's mission, assist in future planning to do that and most of all, how your talents and skills will – you know this by now - **save the company money or make the company money**.

This chapter is not a detailed study of how to ace those tricky questions you've heard some interviewers use these days. Nor is it a long treatise on body language, handshake techniques and other sure-fire

129

approaches to a good impression. There are hundreds of books that do that along with advice on handling interviews for specific jobs. If you believe it will help, by all means read one or more. There is also a large amount of such information available on the internet without having to spend a dime. Your call.

What you *will* get from this chapter are some common-sense, easy-to-remember, easy-to-use, stress- and nerve-reducing pointers that will help you present your best, most professional self in any interview situation.

THE TELEPHONE INTEREVIEW

When a resume is good enough to make it through all the obstacles to actually being read by a human, the next step is usually the preliminary telephone interview. The goal is to move forward to the in-person, on-site interview and you need to achieve this by voice alone. Here's how in five easy tactics:

Tactic No. 1: Stand up and smile. Yes, I mentioned this before: get out of your chair and onto your feet for the entire conversation. You will exude energy. Now smile. People can "hear" a smile over the line. It is a standard technique of radio broadcasters when reading copy so the message will be well received on the other end.

You can try this out before that all-important, preliminary interview. Next time someone phones, sit down and frown. Then, stand and smile. Can you see, hear and feel the difference? Your caller can—ask them. Watch someone on the phone speaking to a small child. They're not making all those silly faces for their own benefit—they're doing it for the sonic effect if will have on the baby!

Tactic No. 2: Keep the company's website open on your computer. You knew this call was coming so by the time of the telephone interview, you should be so familiar with this site that you can click through it during the conversation and address any corporate issues that come up.

Tactic No. 3: Print out the job posting and have it in front of you.

This will be a reminder, as you speak, to reference the requirements of the position and better answer the questions of the interview. Have your resume in front of you, as well as your Accomplishments/Achievements worksheet, so you can refer to the achievements and accomplishments that obviously got the interviewer's attention for this particular interview.

Tactic No. 4: Keep your questions and answers short. Answer each question clearly, and then wait for the interviewer to move on. The purpose of this conversation is to determine if you are worth the time and expense involved in a face-to-face interview, so answer succinctly and try to gauge how much to say and how much to hold back. Answer the questions fully, but try to retain some of the details of your achievements. You might say, "I look forward to telling you exactly how I did that when we meet in person." Save the broader conversation for the on-site interview.

Tactic No. 5: Send a thank-you email. If, by the time of the telephone interview, you do not have the recruiter's or hiring manager's email address, ask for it. Then, whether you are told to expect a follow-up interview from another person, have an appointment to interview in-person, or even if you have been *disqualified from any further consideration*, send a thank-you email within 15 or 20 minutes of finishing the call. (I clearly recognize that being disqualified from consideration may not put you in the best frame of mind for a "thank you" but those other "more qualified" individuals interviewed and offered the job could still bomb due to any number of reasons such as background checks or not accepting the company's offer. Your thank you note may be the catalyst for a recruiter calling you back.)

In your email, explain how you feel you can fit into the organization and that you are certain you can "add shareholder value" or "save the organization money." You know the mantra by now, and how to use it.

Thank you notes are good business and they can make the difference between being remembered and being forgotten.

THE IN-PERSON INTERVIEW

To begin with the obvious, dress professionally. If you are long out of school and skipped the entry-level resume chapter, here's a reminder I gave the "kids" that you should know too: people fundamentally like to hire people who look like they do. This has nothing to do with race or age or gender and has everything to do with that magical first impression. So make sure it's the right first impression - dress appropriately.

Following are high points to keep in mind that will help you succeed in any interview.

NERVES

You got the interview, which is more than most people who sent a resume, did. Don't forget that. No matter how nervous you are (nervousness is understandable and all interviewers know that) you were *asked* to be here. They *want* to see you. They believe you have something to offer their company. Let that knowledge help relax you a bit.

CREATE A DIALOGUE

You got the interview because you are an expert. You have the skills needed to fill this position and your goal now is to create a conversation, a give-and-take that will reveal your professional credentials and ability to succeed in the job.

As much as the job in question allows for such, offer yourself up as a *consultant*. Be prepared to discuss this opportunity as an equal with your interviewer and don't be shy about asking your own questions. The more you can steer the interview toward a dialogue rather than a stiff Q and A, the better.

BE YOURSELF

Smile, be as natural as you can under the circumstances and maintain eye contact with the interviewer at all times. Really listen to the interviewer with your whole being and answer questions as forthrightly and honestly as you can. Listening well and responding appropriately is almost never done well (most people are thinking about what they will say next) and your interviewer will take positive notice.

REMEMBER THE REALLY USEFUL JOB SEARCH TACTICS MANTRA AND USE IT

As much as is reasonable without going overboard, relate the REALLY Useful Job Search Tactics mantra: you are here to **make the company money or save the company money.** Depending on the type of position you are interviewing for, that could be a discussion of increasing shareholder value, reducing man-hours spent on a manufacturing operation, adding value to the organization or saving time - whatever is appropriate.

This is key to interview success yet no recruiter I have ever spoken with has ever heard such language from a job applicant. Back in Chapter 3, I told you about the staffing director who, had never heard "I am here to add shareholder value" in his 33 years on the job. Don't be like all the others!

You will turn yourself into a compelling choice for an employer by addressing the company's needs and goals each and every time you see an appropriate opening.

"I WANT THIS JOB"

If the interview has gone well and the job is a good fit for you, stand up at the end of your interview, offer your hand, look the recruiter in the eye and say: "I want this job." In "salesman speak", ask for the order. This is a very powerful statement - so don't say it unless you mean it.

Alternately, if during the interview you realize the job is not for you, it is reasonable to politely say so and take an early leave. Just so the effort isn't a complete loss, think of it as a practice session and replay the interview for yourself later. Take note of what went well, what was good about your presentation, what wasn't and what you can do better next time.

INTERVIEW DON'TS

These are fairly obvious, but too many job applicants don't heed this advice.

Don't No. 1: Do not ask about vacations, time off, sick days or holiday schedules. That makes the interview all about "me, me, me" and not about the company and how you can **make them money or save them money.** Speak to their mission and goals and the rest will work itself out.

Don't No. 2: Don't look at your watch. In fact, leave it at home. When you are at a job interview, you have nowhere else to be and the recruiter gets every ounce of your attention.

Don't No. 3: Don't allow your cell phone to ring. There is nothing more unprofessional (let-me-show-you-to-the-door unprofessional!) than your cell phone ringing during an interview. In fact, leave it in the car. If you arrived by train or subway, turn it off. That's *off*, not vibrate. If there is anyone in your life more important at that moment than your recruiter, you shouldn't be there.

Don't No. 4: Don't ask about money. Salary and benefits are important. In fact, they are crucial in deciding to take a particular job. But they are not yours to ask about until it has been established that you are a finalist for the position, which, sometimes takes more than one interview.

The single exception to "Don't Rule No. 4" occurs if you have somehow gotten as far as the in-person interview without knowing the range of the salary offer. You do have a right to know that you are reasonably within the ballpark, but keep the question in your pocket until well into the interview. If the range is satisfactory, you then must wait until you have passed all the auditions, and then allow the company to begin the salary discussions. This may not be easy, but it's their game and you are required to play by their rules.

Defensible Statements

Remember "defensible statements" from Chapter 2—those responsibilities you haven't taken on yet, but that you know you are capable of? The in-person interview is the time to make these known to the recruiter: "I can easily manage a team of 60 people or so," even though you've never been in charge of more than ten.

This is a defensible statement if you are confident about it, particularly if a former supervisor or co-worker, as reference, will agree with it. Don't go overboard, but be firm about speaking to the future and explain why you believe you can do this.

ILLEGAL QUESTIONS

There are some questions that federal and local law has determined cannot be asked of job candidates. With certain exceptions, these include marital status, whether you have children, your religion and some others.

If you are offended by a question you believe is illegal or inappropriate, you have several choices:

- Terminate the interview and leave
- Ask for a supervisor to report the incident
- Courteously but firmly ask the interviewer the reason for asking, stating that it is your understanding the question is not allowed by law
- Answer the question and continue the interview

What you decide to do depends on your personal need and inclination – how interested you are in the position, how badly you need the job, your tolerance for confrontation, and your level of militancy in the face of unfairness. It's up to you.

THANK YOU LETTERS

I once made a hire based purely on a thank-you letter. Before email (to the young people among us, yes, there was a time when written communication was done by snail mail), the thank you letter was sent immediately upon returning home from a job interview. Although many job applicants skip that ritual, it is a REALLY Useful Job Search Tactics requirement.

In the case of my hire, all three candidates were essentially identical in capability and professionalism, but only one sent a personalized thank you letter. That sealed the deal.

Today, with email, instant messenger, Blackberries, etc. thank you notes are expected to arrive more quickly than in the past. This is, of course, even more critical if you believe the hiring decision will be made immediately. There is no social stigma attached to an email thank you. Do it.

Your email should be short and to the point.

Dear _____,

Thank you for your time and professional consideration.
I am the1 right person for the _____ position and will contribute to the bottom line. I look forward to hearing from you soon.

Sincerely,
Jerry Jobseeker
123.456.7890 – home
098.765.4321 – mobile
jerry@his&domain.com

Yes, include "Dear" - even in an email. Also include your telephone number(s) and email address. Don't make it difficult for an employer to contact you.

A REALLY USEFUL JOB SEARCH TACTICS EXTRA

Here's a tactic that will make you memorable even if the recruiter has interviewed tens of people in the past three days:

Carry with you to interviews some small, blank, panel cards and bring matching envelopes. You can find these in any office supply store. Be sure you have more than one to cover for any mistakes.

When you reach the lobby after an interview, take a minute – it won't take more than twice that long – to handwrite a thank you note *on the spot*. Place it in an envelope with the recruiter's name written on it, and ask the receptionist to deliver it to Mr. or Ms. Recruiter right away.

Think this won't make you a star? It's how to make a real-time impression while you are still fresh in the mind of your interviewer. Don't let them forget you!

REALLY Useful Job Search Tactic #30:

STAND AND SMILE FOR YOUR TELEPHONE INTERVIEWS.

REALLY Useful Job Search Tactic #31:

USE THE REALLY USEFUL JOB SEARCH TACTICS MANTRA IN YOUR INTERVIEW: MAKE YOU MONEY/SAVE YOU MONEY.

REALLY Useful Job Search Tactic #32:

THANK YOU NOTES ARE MANDATORY VIA EMAIL, SNAIL MAIL, OR TO REALLY MAKE AN IMPRESSION, RIGHT ON THE SPOT!.

WHAT HAVE YOU GOT
AGAINST STAFFING COMPANIES?
(And, for the record, I'm not in the staffing business)

"Everybody has talent; it's just a matter of moving around until you've discovered what it is."

-George Lucas

 SOME QUICK STAFFING STATS

- 2.9 million people are employed daily by staffing companies.
- Staffing companies have created 530,000 new jobs over the past two years.
- 82% of temporary and contract employees work full time, virtually the same as the rest of the work force.

Source: American Staffing Association, 9/2006
www.americanstaffing.net

To a large degree, job seekers have a jaded view of staffing companies and I want to ask "What have you got against staffing companies and why does it matter from whom you get your next job?" According to the numbers above, approximately 10% of the US population is employed by the staffing industry on a *daily* basis!

To be fair to the job seeker, a lot of negative perceptions people have of staffing companies were created as a result of business practices personnel companies employed (pun intended) prior to the mid 1980's or so. Particularly, the practice of job seekers paying for their jobs. This was customary for many years. Thirty, 40, 50, and up to 70% of a few months or a full year's worth of salary (!) was not an uncommon fee for a job seeker to pay for a staffing company's services. If you haven't been in the job market for twenty years or more and you previously signed on with and paid an agency for a job, this may be the only reason you are not inclined to interview with a staffing company.

Things have changed. Unless you engage a career coach or an executive headhunter to work exclusively on your behalf, you should not be paying fees to anyone for their job procurement services. The company that hires you will be responsible for paying the freight.

Regardless of how many jobs they may fill, how many people they employ, or how many opportunities staffing companies offer, they still suffer from a negative public opinion of the industry as a whole. Let's address a couple of the impressions the public has of staffing companies.

NOTE: If you have a low opinion of staffing companies, *keep it to yourself.* Numerous corporations retain staffing companies to perform their on-site recruiting duties. Even though performing the duties of the host company, and appearing to be employees of the host company, they are actually employed by the staffing company. This is not the time to say something disparaging of staffing companies because you happen to notice a staffing company logo on the calendar, notepad and coffee cup. Don't assume they were left there by a salesperson! Thought you ought to know before you go.

PUBLIC IMPRESSION # 1: IT TAKES TOO LONG TO GET IN AND OUT OF AN AGENCY

This one may depend on your definition of what "too long" is when you recognize that somebody is willing to go to work on your behalf. It will take time to get in and out of an agency and there are good reasons why. To help, call ahead and schedule an appointment. When you arrive, don't become upset if your appointment time gets moved some. It happens all the time and it's just the nature of the business. Dealing with people takes time and you will expect the same focused attention when it's your turn.

THE APPLICATION

You can expect to be required to fill out an application. Yes, you have done a wonderful job with your Superior Resume (which you have with you) but a staffing company will not want it...not yet. Instead, you will be asked to complete an application.

The application will ask for a lot of information that will not be on your resume. To speed up the application process, prepare in advance a comprehensive list of names, phone numbers, addresses, previous employers, references, etc. It's much more professional than asking for the phone book or using your cell phone to call personal references for their information. Arrive organized. Show the agency that you are prepared, serious and diligent about getting a job. They notice this stuff - they are evaluating you from the minute you hit the front door.

Although this information is vital for the agency to do their best for you, the primary purpose of an agency application is as a legal document. The in-house application will provide you with statements of responsibility from the company to you, your responsibilities to them, your *required* permission to obtain and disclose personal information, permission to contact previous employers and references as well as statements of pay, benefits and more. It is extremely important that you read and understand this document. It is a legal, binding contract and the basis for which both parties will move forward.

THE INTERVIEW

You will be interviewed. No staffing company will, in any manner, act on behalf of an individual they are not comfortable representing. Understand that recruiters who staff agencies are among the best when it comes to interviewing. Staffing companies train continuously and strive to operate on the cutting edge of behavioral interviewing techniques. This is one of the key elements they offer their customers—the ability to ascertain, via these interviewing techniques (among other means), that the candidate they promote to their client match predetermined criteria in every way possible. "Every way possible" includes much more than just the ability to do the job. It also includes such intangibles as personalities, culture and the on-site chemistry of all parties concerned.

Pay attention while at the staffing company. Listen and learn the process. You should treat your staffing interview as practice—it is - don't treat it lightly. This is a real opportunity to fine-tune your interviewing skills.

TESTING

Another time consideration that you will have to deal with is skill and aptitude testing. Think you are too good, experienced or professional to be tested? Forget it. You will be tested. Once again the company has to know that you can really "walk the walk" and they will verify that you can. Do it with a smile. You might learn something!

***

Starting to see where all your time has gone? You may be thinking all this to be unreasonable but think about it from the staffing company's point of view. They have to pay staff; provide training, facilities, and equipment; conduct expensive and specialized testing and pay sales people to hit the street in order to help you get your job. All this time and money has been spent to meet you, learn about you, and make the determination that you could be the candidate they recognize as the right person to fill an order they may have just received. They are creating an investment in you.

Are you inventory? You bet! And you have to be the very best inventory they have to offer their clients in order for you to get a job (and for them to make a buck!). You (and your agency) are always competing. And keep in mind that you become your agency's reputation when you go out on an interview. You represent that company whether you are interviewing for a permanent position or a single day's work as a clerical temp.

PUBLIC IMPRESSION #2: THE STAFFING COMPANY DOESN'T HAVE ANY JOBS

This is a regular complaint of staffing companies and there may be some truth in it. It's not likely to be the case with the major, highly recognized names you may interview with but no one can speak for smaller operations you encounter. You might want to do a little investigative work prior to making an appointment with any staffing company. Visit their website and view the number and quality of ads posted. If they don't suit your interests, move on.

INTERVIEW WITH ALL STAFFING COMPANIES

The REALLY Useful Job Search Tactics approach to staffing companies? If you apply with one, apply with them all. Plan two a day - one in the morning and one in the afternoon—until you have interviewed with all companies who may have any possible value to your job search. Remember, *you* don't pay anything for a staffing company's time!

No staffing company/temporary agency can offer the entire world. You must apply to all agencies—at least in the beginning. Once you determine which one(s) will keep you employed (if you are temping), you may want to discontinue any relationships with others - but not till then. No agency is "working" for you even though they represent you. This may be a fine distinction but understand that their client company pays for their services.

And speaking of the corporate client, major corporations regularly retain more than one staffing company to handle their account. Your problem, if you want to work for Major Corporation, is that you need to be registered with at least one of their staffing agencies and you won't know which have working agreements. You're only option? Each staffing company must be familiar with you and your resume. (I did say two a day!)

Don't worry if two or more of the agencies you interview with send your identical resume over for consideration to Major Corporation. That is of no concern to you. If you utilize the services of more than one staffing company, a REALLY Useful Job Search Tactic I strongly advise, you should hope that just such an occurrence would take place.

Back to the idea that staffing companies don't have any jobs. "All they want is my resume as inventory so that when a job comes up they have something on file to submit." This, unfortunately, can occur - which is why you must do your due diligence by visiting a company's website and calling the office and do your own investigation. Don't be shy about contacting them. Ask questions such as how many positions they have filled this month and in the past 3 months. Ask how long they have been in business. Take the time to learn all you can about any staffing company you determine may be able to offer you the jobs and support you seek.

THE GOOD STUFF A STAFFING COMPANY WILL DO FOR YOU

We have pretty much figured out that staffing companies are in it for the money. Great! Isn't that what this is all about? And because of the profit motive, staffing companies will do something for you that I can't begin to offer you in this book and you can't receive from any networking group anywhere no matter how good they may be: The staffing company will prepare you with a thorough pre-interview of the kind only they can provide.

This preparation will give you the confidence to shine in a new environment. You are coached with information relevant to the position you are interviewing for and the company. You will have advance knowledge of the parties you will be meeting. They may even be able to provide you with some "slippery slopes" to shy away from. You will be told beforehand of a company's culture and other intimate information that a candidate walking in from the street has no knowledge of. All this gives you an advantage.

Do not take all of this pre-prep from the staffing company to mean that you can shirk your responsibility for being prepared. If you are leaving straight from the staffing company to go to your interview (very common), ask for time to go online to make yourself familiar with your potential employer's website. This time spent may provide you with one little nugget of information valuable to your interview.

A SPECIAL DISCUSSION ON TEMPORARY AGENCIES

Depending on a variety of circumstances, you may be a prime candidate for temporary (temp) work. Your personal schedule or circumstances may not allow you time to work "traditional" hours. For many job seekers, there may be excellent reasons to consider temp work as a career lifestyle or as - pun intended - a *temporary* employment measure.

TESTING THE WATERS

A short-term job can be an opportunity to test the waters of a company you've been interested in, or the sort of work you may be considering transitioning to. A temp assignment will give you an excellent feel for the environment and ambience of a corporation, their style of management, the conditions of employment. And, you never know when a temporary job might introduce you to a new kind of work you've never considered before, something you could be quite good at and enjoy enormously. Surprises come in many different packages and a job you've taken that you originally accepted as a "filler" could lead to a life-long career.

PART-TIME TEMPORARY JOBS

There are many instances in life when full-time work is not feasible or even possible. Perhaps you're a professional mom or dad who needs a short-term cash infusion. Or, you're a full-time student who can work only during school breaks. Maybe you need a job to help make ends meet while you're shopping a business plan for your dream corporation. Or you are an artist who needs enough cash now and again to cover the rent so you can concentrate on your work for a few months uninterrupted. In any of these circumstances, part time temporary jobs can be an ideal solution.

TRANSITIONING CAREERS

You've noticed that more factories, offices and stores are shutting down in your chosen industry rather than expanding. Or, you're burnt out, can barely drag yourself to work each day, having lost interest in a career that you once thought would make you a star. And, maybe, you just don't like what you do every day to put food on the table.

Any of these scenarios calls for a career change, and it is an ideal situation in which to investigate possible new careers or gain experience in one you're attracted to through temporary work assignments.

It's not easy. No temp agency will send you on a job you can't do so you will often be transferring skills to new uses, or starting at the bottom to gain new skills. And without experience or credentials in the new job or field, you'll be paid less than you're accustomed to.

But if you are determined to make an employment/career change (or forced into it due to economic circumstances beyond your control), a temp agency is often the best option to help you toward a new goal.

BENEFITS

Today more corporations are staffing with independent contractors. These are full-time jobs, but they come with no medical coverage, no paid vacations or holidays and none of the other benefits that for decades were part of an employment package. Some companies have cut back benefits so steeply they hardly exist.

But many staffing agencies, large and small, provide these benefits and even, sometimes, bonus incentives. When you take a temp job with Giant Chemical, you work on their premises under their supervision, but the temp agency that sent you there is your legal employer and is responsible for paying you. They are acting as your agent, supplying your services to Giant Chemical, whom they will bill for those services, including the cost of your benefits.

As with most permanent jobs, these benefits won't kick in until you have achieved a certain number of hours on the job. But, since fewer and fewer permanent jobs come with the benefits they once did, sometimes a temporary agency may be a good full-time alternative, particularly for workers with children.

FREE AGENCY

There is another kind of temporary work called free agency in which you work for yourself. You offer your skills on the open market through your own networking and, frequently, through such websites as Elance.com where temporary, freelance jobs are listed and you can bid on them. What sets Free Agency apart from other types of temp or contract work is that you may spend 6 hours Monday working for Chet in Omaha because that is all the time he needs with an accountant each week. Then Tuesday you may be contracted to work with Ronnie in San Diego for 4 hours. You may be contracted to work one day a week, 2 days a month, etc. It's a very interesting and growing concept.

This kind of contract/temp arrangement applies almost exclusively to work that can be done in offices or home (as opposed to say, a welder who needs travel to a location or work in an established shop), generally requires extensive computer skills and can be delivered electronically or by mail service. The assignments, though technically temporary, can sometimes run as long as two or three years and occasionally they become permanent positions.

WHEN TEMPORARY BECOMES PERMANENT

As I explained in the beginning of this book, anyone who is employed is nothing more than a line item in this year's budget. Temping is no different except that when the job is complete, you will be looking for work again and your agency has, or is searching out, another opportunity for you.

Quite often though, a temporary employee is asked to stay on with the company as a permanent member of the staff. This may be the one time in your life as a job seeker when the negotiating tables are reversed. In this instance, it is *you* doing the interviewing, *you* seeking information that will convince you to take the job or not and *you* who may be able to demand a minimum contract guaranteeing your employment for a set period of time along with a compensation payment in the event of earlier termination.

***

Temporary workers receive far more respect today as more people see the value in taking on temporary assignments, either short- or long-term, as a needed filler between "real" jobs or as a career of choice. Either way, take this style of work as seriously as standard employment. Keep the REALLY Useful Job Search Tactics mantra in mind – **Save Your Employer Money/Make Your Employer Money** – when you are working with temporary agencies. They will work with you and around your schedule to get the assignments you need or want if they believe you are one of their premiere candidates.

ALL KINDS OF STAFFING COMPANIES

There are as many types of staffing companies, as there are types of employment. There are industry-specific agencies; general, full service agencies; permanent placement and temporary agencies; medical and accounting agencies; hospitality and sales agencies and on and on. For just about any category you can name, there is an agency in existence to serve it specifically. There are even staffing companies that place people in, yep - staffing agencies! Take the time to call ahead and know what type of staffing company you are preparing to spend your valuable time with before you arrive.

***

It is common that job seekers find themselves in a position that they would have not been able to obtain on their own, receiving higher pay and benefits than they may have anticipated and working in a more challenging and satisfying job than they had thought possible—all due to the efforts of their staffing company.

So, once again I ask: what have you got against staffing companies?

REALLY Useful Job Search Tactic #33:

IF YOU UTILIZE THE SERVICES OF ONE STAFFING COMPANY, THEN USE THE SERVICES OF ALL STAFFING COMPANIES IN YOUR NEIGHBORHOOD, YOUR CITY, AND/OR YOUR INDUSTRY!

REALLY Useful Job Search Tactic #34:

TEMPORARY OR PART TIME EMPLOYMENT OR FREE AGENCY, DEPENDING ON YOUR PERSONAL CIRCUMSTANCES, TRAINING, AND ABILITY, MAY OPEN DOORS AND EMPLOYMENT OPPORTUNITIES THAT YOU MAY NOT KNOW EXIST.

Job Farming or Finding The Jobs Less Apparent

"Those who do not create the future they want must endure the future they get."
- Admiral Draper L. Kaufman, Jr.

In the residential real estate business, a common form of launching a career is to "farm" your territory (your neighborhood) by informing everyone you come in contact with that you are in the real estate business and ready to go to work for them. How is this done? By going door-to-door, by direct mail to each address within an eight- or ten-square-block area, and by becoming an expert in the market that is your chosen territory.

The same technique applies to "job farming," a technique for finding those jobs that are not apparent.

The easiest job postings to find are the ones listed in the Sunday paper and at online job boards. So being, they are also the ones every other job seeker is responding to, irregardless of their qualifications, and the jobs for which there is the most competition. If that is the only effort you make, you are missing 60 to 80 percent of available jobs—but you already know this.

As discussed in Chapter 9, networking is one way to find some of these positions and many succeed using this technique. But it is still a passive activity that is dependent on others remembering you or remembering to pass on your card or telephone number. So it is important that unless you are willing to wait on the job you're finally offered, you need to become proactive. That means learning to "drill down" for the jobs less apparent. Here's how.

THE BUSINESS JOURNAL

You've prepared your REALLY Useful Job Search Tactics Superior Resume and it's ready to go at a moment's notice. You respond to job listings anywhere you can find them. And you seek every opportunity to network. Good. But if you are truly serious, the following technique will teach you how to find jobs that *other people won't locate*. It is admittedly a little more time consuming, but so what? You have time! It requires diligent effort on your part - but you are a diligent person. Let's get to work!

Most large cities in the United States have weekly business journals. The largest publisher of such journals is American City Business Journals (*www.bizjournals.com*), whose publications include The Houston Business Journal, The San Antonio Business Journal, The Los Angeles Business Journal and dozens of others with such city names. Other, similar magazines in your area may be independent, associated with local newspapers or local chambers of commerce. They all count.

As a subscriber to the Houston Business Journal, I receive their annual Book of Lists, which, along with the telephone book, is one of the best sources of sales leads available. The book of lists for your city is available at your local Chamber of Commerce office and, probably, at your local library as well as bookstore magazine sections or directly from the publisher.

Yes, I know, I said "sales leads." What does that mean to you as a job seeker?

The Book of Lists is one of the greatest sources of *job* leads of all time, and hardly anyone uses it. Here is why it is so valuable to you:

The Book of Lists, as compiled by the American City Business

Journals, is an annual publication that collects in one place the lists their weekly business newspapers have published each week throughout the previous year. Such lists as:

- Largest Title Companies
- Largest Women-Owned Businesses
- The Top 25 Mechanical Engineering Firms

And many more. At least one list is published weekly and sometimes as many as 5 or 6, so the annual compilation is, at minimum, 52 lists (for a small market) to hundreds (in a large city or metro area).

The entry for each company on each list generally includes such information as the name of the CEO, the number of employees, the dollar volume in sales of products or services the company provides as well as local addresses, websites and phone numbers.

Now, all you need to do (he said with a grin) is to contact each and every company listed in each and every category of interest to you. This task is time-consuming and will take some concerted effort, but I promise, it isn't difficult.

First, find the book of lists in your city. Next, identify those categories of professional interest to you. As an example, let's say you are an information technology guy who would like to work inside a law firm.

The Houston Business Journal Book of Lists offers this listing: "Largest Houston-Area Law Firms (Ranked by the Number of Local Lawyers)." There are 25 firms on the list – some of them world-class - and you know that each one has a superb, well-staffed information technology department that sooner or later will need your skills.

So your job now is to telephone each firm, ask for the director of IT and open with the scripted lines I have prepared for you below.

Don't plan on snagging an interview with your first call (although it has been known to happen), but do plan to make a valuable contact for future networking. What you want to achieve in this first run at the company is:

1. Get a name and make a personal contact with someone you can speak with in the future and

2. Get your resume to this person even if there is nothing available at this time.

Remember, this is the person who recognizes the need, then creates and fills the IT department's positions. He or she is also the person who will obtain salary budget approval – the person you need to know. Here's how you do it:

Prepare a one- or two-line script. During the conversation, keep the REALLY Useful Job Search Tactics mantra, **Save You Money/Make You Money**, in mind. Don't force it but if the opportunity arrives, let your listener know that you will, in this case, save them money. Here are sample scripts:

Sample Script No. 1

Hi, My name is _____ and I am a _____(Your Job Title or Job Description)_____professional. I am seeking an opportunity to work in a major law firm, maybe even a contract opportunity and, quite frankly, I have a lot to offer my next employer. Would you have time I could visit in person to discuss my resume (or "qualifications", if you prefer.)

If you get a "yes", set the appointment. If you think you can pull it off, offer to buy coffee to get the person out of the office and onto neutral territory and away from the phone.

If you're told there are no openings, no time, etc. follow up with this:

Sample Script No. 2

I completely understand. Can I forward my resume so that you will have it when an opening comes available?

(And lastly) Any chance you may know of any opportunities at any other law firms in town?

The goal here is to get an email address and make a friend. Then you have a handy way to drop a line every few weeks or couple of months (even after you have found a job) to keep yourself at the top of the potential employee list in a hiring manager's mind. And, if all else fails, always go for the referral. Remember that like-employed individuals often run into each other at luncheons, continuing education classes, conferences, association meetings and such.

After you've finished that telephone call, move on to the second law firm on the list, then the third and so on.

Admittedly, this is tedious. It's also what the *most successful of salespeople* do in one manner or other. Consider this: if you are diligent and you get the name of the director or vice president of IT for each of the 25 law firms, you have 25 contacts who hire people with your skills and with that many, there are bound to be several openings you will be hearing of soon.

If that many calls seems overwhelming, think of it this way: if you make one call a day, you will have made contact with each of those 25 major law firms in just five weeks. If you call only *five* a day, in one week you could be deciding which target list from the book of lists to attack next. If you make 25 calls a day....

Job farming requires concerted effort, but at this point in time, job farming – job seeking *is* your job! If you create a calling plan, stick with it and follow up with the contacts you've made, the payoff could very well be your dream job - without ever having to deal with the competition that happens as a result of all the published job listings everyone else is reading.

Now this is networking!

REALLY Useful Job Search Tactic #35:

JOB SEEKING *IS* YOUR JOB!
BECOME AGGRESSIVELY INVOLVED IN "JOB FARMING" AND
ANTICIPATE GETTING THE CALL WHILE OTHER JOB SEEKERS ARE
WONDERING WHAT TO DO WITH THEIR TIME.

Pre-Employment Assessments, Tests and Checks

"Experience is not what happens to you;
it's what you do with what happens to you."
- Aldous Huxley

Pre-employment tests and checks are almost universal now; most employers use some if not all of them. They can be expensive, so when you are asked to submit to them, you know you are in serious contention for the job.

The tests and checks fall into six categories, which I'll cover one-by-one: assessments, skills tests, background checks, credit checks, drug tests and previous employer inquiries.

ASSESSMENTS

Assessments can reveal a lot about a person when they are reviewed by someone with substantial training in interpreting the results. They usually cover such aspects of character as personality, honesty, aptitude, intelligence and cultural fit. Ultimately, they are designed to predict a candidate's likely success at a given position.

Opinions on pre-employment assessments range from "no one should ever be hired without a psychologically-based assessment" to "all pre-employment assessments should be against the law." Some people question the ethics and legality of these assessments, issues that are not within the scope of this book. REALLY Useful Job Search Tactics will not take a stance either way.

If you need advice concerning whether or not an assessment is legal, consult an attorney.

The one point that is not in question, however, is that an employer may not cherry-pick candidates for assessment. The law requires – in all states - that all candidates for a specific job be tested equally. That is to say that if a salesperson is tested for sales ability, *all* sales candidates must be given the same test. Note that I did not say *all* candidates applying to *every* job at a company are required to undergo testing. The assessment that was developed to determine a salesperson's ability to overcome obstacles and close the sale will have no value testing, say, a graphic artist. An artist will go to work based on his or her portfolio and is not likely to be put through a "graphic artist's assessment".

For companies that use assessments for a particular position, they are not optional. If you are asked and you want the job, you are going to take the test.

Most assessments are comprised of multiple-choice questions and are timed. It won't take you long to realize you are being repeatedly asked the "same" questions in different forms. This redundancy is intended to determine consistency, which is key to a successful result.

Because assessments basically test who you are when you walk in the door, you cannot study for them and there is no pass or fail. You are what you are, so there is no point in trying to game the exam. Just be honest and go with your first impulse.

***

All that said, understand that if you are asked to take one, do it. You have nothing to lose and a lot to gain (if you get the job). As I said earlier, there is no "studying" for such an assessment.

Because there are *so* many companies that offer assessments, the quality varies and can be hard to, well, assess (sorry!). It has been my experience that every person wandering the streets with a master's degree in psychology has an assessment of some sort tucked away somewhere. That is not to say that there are not some highly reputable companies that offer this service. Success rates determine if an assessment company will remain in business and success is why companies continue to assess prospective employees. Any tool that may prove out an employee's potential value to a company before they start work - well, you get the picture.

SKILLS TESTING

Unlike assessments, skills tests measure knowledge and capability ranging from a standard typing test to such specialized skills as drafting, mechanical abilities and trade-specific skills. These are tests you *can* fail and no one argues their validity, particularly when the job can affect the health and safety of others, such as a journeyman electrician or commercial vehicle operator.

In the case of these tests, you had better be able to deliver on the claims you made on your resume. And don't think someone of your experience and position shouldn't be tested on skills you left behind years ago in your career advancement. Some companies, as a matter of policy, require all candidates at every level to test out on Microsoft Word or Excel, for example. Even if you'll never use an Excel spreadsheet in your job, don't protest and do the best you can. Sometimes you're not being graded on the skill as such, but on your ability to be a team player and get along with others.

BACKGROUND INVESTIGATIONS

Hardly anyone gets hired these days without a background check. It's all about risk and liability, the due diligence necessary for corporations to avoid exposing themselves to catastrophic lawsuits. Background checks (and don't forget the Google "background search") are an inexpensive way to acquire such "insurance" and there is the possibility of discovering a history of behavior that could adversely affect an employee's performance or negatively affect the business. No one needs a convicted embezzler working as the company controller.

If there is anything in your background that might raise an eyebrow, you cannot reasonably just hope it won't be discovered. Bring it up during the interview process after you begin to get the idea you have a real shot at this job because, even if it is something that is later determined to be of small or no concern, when you are found to have concealed the truth, it will work against you. Somewhere along the line, you signed a document attesting to the truth of your statements. If that is proved otherwise, go home. Game over.

If you're embarrassed about a past misadventure, remember that Human Resources has seen and heard it all. Chances are that if you are truthful and don't set up a recruiter to be embarrassed later for not knowing, you can still be considered for the job.

It can be more difficult if you have in your past a significantly negative incident. You may do better at finding employment through one of the larger staffing companies, some of which have sources for jobs where a poor background is of lesser importance than the ability to perform. Overall, it is incumbent on you to be forthcoming and truthful.

CREDIT CHECKS

To the job seeker, credit checks are a touchy issue in relation to employment. Why should a potential employer be able to view such personal information as your credit and purchasing history, and is it really relevant? Evidently it is. Many companies believe that a good financial history correlates with a responsible employee and that people with clean financial records are less likely to be a problem.

But - and this is important - a prospective employer may not access your credit history without your permission. You may not have noticed, but somewhere during the application process, you probably signed an authorization for the company to obtain your credit report. This one permission also gives them the right, *for as long as you remain on the payroll,* to recheck your credit history at any time. It could make a difference between a promotion and being passed over if your credit rating does not pass muster in the future.

Somewhere between 35 and 50 percent of companies now perform pre-employment credit checks; so if you have had financial problems in the past and learn a credit check is part of the hiring process, address the issue with your interviewer. Be sure to mention it if your difficulties are mitigated by a medical situation or other sudden catastrophe. And if you have had a pristine financial background in the past, but are having problems due to your current lack of employment, tell the interviewer of any negative information they may find on your credit report. The key here is to be proactive; let them know that you have nothing to hide.

If you aren't sure what your credit report looks like, take the time to find out. It is not uncommon to find mistakes that can reflect negatively on you. There are three major credit bureaus: Experian, TransUnion and Equifax, and federal law allows everyone one free copy of their credit report every year. You can find out how to obtain yours at the bureaus' websites or by telephoning them directly.

Pre-employment credit checks must be done within the guidelines of the Fair Credit Reporting Act (FCRA). Interestingly, this legislation requires that if a company obtained your permission to purchase your credit report and doesn't hire you because of an adverse credit report, they must notify you *twice*: once when the decision is *being made* (huh?) and the second time after you have been rejected for the job. Here is how the General Services Administration words this requirement:

> *"Before you reject an applicant based on credit report information, you must make a pre-adverse action disclosure that includes a copy of the credit report and the summary of consumer rights under the FCRA. Once you've rejected an applicant, you must provide an adverse action notice if credit report information affected your decision."*

You can learn more at this government website: *http://www.pueblo. gsa.gov.* Search "Fair Credit Reporting Act".

DRUG TESTING

Pre-employment drug testing laws are different in every state. Some allow tests for any occupation; others only for specific occupations (such as commercial driving); and still others disallow testing at all.

If you have questions about your state's practices, you can get information from your state employment agency. If your state allows drug tests and you are asked to take one as a pre-employment (or continuing employment) requirement, you have no choice.

PREVIOUS EMPLOYERS

In general these days, corporations will issue only the blandest statement about a previous employee: "she is eligible for re-hire/he is not eligible for re-hire." That's it. If you can get a former supervisor to speak in your behalf as a personal reference, you are ahead of the game, but don't count on it. Many are banned by company policy from speaking with your potential new employer at all.

BOTTOM LINE

If you interviewed today and started work tomorrow, you are either setting a land speed record or you are 16 years old with no work experience to verify yet. Tests, assessments and checks are the way of working life today and there is no way to avoid them. Given corporate fear of exposure and liability, all these pre-employment obstacles will only become more sophisticated as time goes by. Your job is to be as knowledgeable as you reasonably can about "people assessing tools" and then cooperate to the best of your ability and with good cheer.

<u>REALLY Useful Job Search Tactic #36:</u>

SUBMIT TO PRE-EMPLOYMENT ASSESSMENTS AND SKILLS TESTING AGREEABLY. YOU CAN'T PREPARE OR STUDY FOR THEM, SO JUMP IN WITH BOTH FEET AND DO YOUR BEST.

"Consulting" or Consulting

"A friendship founded on business is a good deal better than a business founded on friendship."
- John D. Rockefeller

If you are reading this book, you probably aren't *really* interested in becoming an independent consultant. On the other hand, if you are the adventurous kind or if you are a mature job seeker whose job search has gone on too long, it has probably been suggested that you become a consultant. This is not necessarily bad advice.

"CONSULTING"

Now, I know that if starting your own business were your goal, you wouldn't necessarily be reading this book. You'd be studying the market in the area of your expertise, making lists of potential clients and setting up shop – perhaps in your basement. So let's call this kind of "consulting" what it really is for you: looking for a job.

That may sound just a little sneaky, but it is not. It is a tactic I promote to use "consulting" time to search for salaried work. Passing out your consulting business cards and taking on short-term jobs is just a personal form of free agency or temping. The only difference is that you are going about acquiring your next job sans an employment agency.

"Consulting" is an excellent opportunity to learn more about your business, yourself, your community, make new networking connections, and it is not unlikely that in time you'll get that job offer you want when someone admires your work and takes you on permanently. As a bonus, your "consultancy" provides you the necessary information to fill in that gap in your resume. It doesn't matter if it took you five months of downtime before you got your first consulting job; you describe the entire time as consulting.

All you need to become a "consultant" – a temporary condition until your next paying job – are business cards, the tools of your trade and a telephone. Friends, former colleagues and your networking skills are your leads to clients. Reread Chapter 9, The Mighty, Mighty Network, for a refresher to get you going.

But what if you get yourself out there on the street, you get a few consulting contracts, they keep coming in and - you love it? It's great to pick and choose whom you work for and do the job on your time, in your way. Maybe you'll like it well enough to turn it into a career. What then?

CONSULTING

Unless you're just out of school, you've got several years to maybe a decade or two of experience. By now, without stretching the point, you could even call yourself an expert. And there are companies out there who don't need your expertise full time or can't afford to pay a full-time employee, but who need your knowledge.

In fact, I know of several successful businesses that began as a result of a worker being laid off, renting an office, installing a phone and computer. It all started when, just as they began marketing themselves, their old employer – the one who had laid them off – called asking if the brand new consultant would consider returning to the old job. Well, no thank you, they said, but having this new business, I'd be glad to consult. That first client who had once been their employer, led to a second, then a third and today, they are all full-fledged small businesses – consultants now employing several other people besides themselves.

WHAT YOU NEED TO KNOW ABOUT BEING A PROFESSIONAL CONSULTANT

If you've been "consulting" for awhile, you already know that you do it all: sales, phone calls, fax, email, fix the computer, keep the books, empty the trash, sweep out the office, the work itself, of course, and perhaps – when things are going really well – juggle several clients at once who all want your undivided attention. Then you catch up with everything else on the weekend. It's astonishing what you can achieve solo in a virtual office especially when you know it's temporary, until the next "real" job comes along. But if you decide to become a consultant (without the quotation marks), *will* you do it all? Can you sustain the pace when it becomes your chosen career?

Let's take a closer look at what you have taken on.

The Market. Before you make the decision to permanently go out on your own, you must verify that you have a viable business, that what you do will still be in demand in three or five or ten years. With the continuing onslaught of new technologies, be sure you are offering a product, service or skill that won't be outdated by some piece of software in the foreseeable future.

Sales. First, you must determine if you are a sales person. Not everyone is or can be. If not, how do you intend to obtain the business you need? Advertising? Trade shows? Referrals? One client, even a big one that pays the bills now, is not enough.

If you don't have sales talent, is there someone who can do it for you? Finding sales people is easy. Finding sales people who are motivated and capable of thinking on their feet is hard, especially for a start-up business.

Good sales people are expensive. If they're really good, they may be snatched away by the competition. Or worse, they may become the competition. One way to head this off is a significant profit-sharing agreement to keep everyone happy and working toward a common goal.

This isn't a book on how to start your own business, but these are a few questions you should consider before you buy such a book.

Managing People. If and when business increases enough to bring on additional people, they will need to be managed. Like sales, this is a skill that not everyone has or wants to do or can learn. And it is different in a small business environment than in a big corporation. These people can't be nine-to-fivers; they need to appreciate and be willing to expend the extra effort a small business takes to succeed.

Employees also cost a lot of money. In addition to their salaries, there is Social Security, Medicare, local, state and federal taxes to withhold and, if you can afford it, health coverage and other benefits. Before you decide, sit down with your accountant and determine how much additional business you need to support the additional people.

Doing Business – The Legal Stuff. I am not an attorney so I cannot advise you on legal questions and besides; every state has its own requirements. If you give your business a name not your own, you may need to file for a DBA (doing business as) certificate. If it is just you, you don't need a Federal ID Number because as a sole proprietor, you can file taxes quarterly under your Social Security Number. Some states, however, may require you to pay a business tax.

Your local chamber of commerce, county clerk or equivalent can advise you on requirements. You may also want to contact the Small Business Administration for business start-up classes (SCORE - Service Core of Retired Executives - at the SBA, has some of the best anywhere) and possible loan guarantee and other financial information.

Being a "consultant" in between salaried jobs is a good way to pick up some temporary work and fill in a hole in your resume. If, however, you have become a consultant, the question of whether to incorporate will eventually become an issue. I can't advise you; only an attorney can. But if you have arrived at that question, you have made the leap. You have determined that you can afford to hire yourself because you can **make yourself money** *and* **save someone else money**. Congratulations! You are now a consultant and a business owner.

REALLLY Useful Job Search Tactic #37:

USE THE "CONSULTING" APPROACH TO FILL IN GAPS IN YOUR RESUME—OR - BECOME A CONSULTANT AND *RUN* YOUR OWN BUSINESS.

ONLINE EMPLOYMENT APPLICATIONS

*"Our Age of Anxiety is, in great part, the result of trying to do today's
jobs with yesterday's tools."*
- Marshall McLuhan

Now that you are, as I've advised, seeking out job listings on the websites
of companies you are interested in working for, it will be very common
to run into online job applications where you won't be able to use your
shiny, new REALLY Useful Job Search Tactics Superior Resume that you
worked so hard to create.

Bummer.

Corporations that use the online application process rarely provide
an email address so you are stuck with entry boxes that will not match the
sections of your resume – most particularly, you can't divide your resume
into the Accomplishments and History sections in online applications.

There is nothing to do but follow their lead. You can, for the most part,
cut and paste the information from your resume into the appropriately
labeled fields. The exception is that your online application employment
history will necessarily be a blend of your "Selected Accomplishments"
and Superior Resume "Employment History". There, you are required
to list previous employment in the traditional resume format. But as
you do so, be thinking in terms of the Superior Resume format. (Is this
getting confusing, yet?) Spice up your 'responsibilities while on the job'

by matching your Selected Achievements to the time and place you achieved them. Remember, I want you to become compelling every time you talk about you! No matter if that may be in your personally created resume or in the body and constraints of an online employment application.

At the end of the online application, there is usually an "Other Information" field. You can use this to include your Objective Statement. Relate it to the specific job posting and speak to what you will be doing for your future employer - how you will **save them money or make them money.**

There are two other fields in online applications that I think merit special consideration.

SOCIAL SECURITY NUMBER

Many online applications provide a field for your Social Security number. **Do not provide this** (always worth repeating)! Identity theft is the fastest-growing crime in the U.S. and all a thief needs to make your life a nightmare for years to come is your name and Social Security number. You already know the drill here. Besides, there is no reason any business needs your Social Security number until they are ready to conduct a background check or cut you a check. Banks and other financial institutions, which are required to report transactions to the federal government, and employers who must report salary and tax information, are the only corporate entities that can, by law, insist upon knowing your Social Security number. But you should not give a *potential* employer your Social Security number.

So, the best thing to do when a Social Security number field appears in the online application form is to skip it. Unfortunately, most online applications cannot be submitted unless all fields are filled. To get around this, try entering a series of X's (xxx-xx-xxxx) or, if the field requires numeric characters, use zeroes (000-00-0000). Sometimes that works, but not always.

If your application is rejected for withholding your Social Security number, telephone the company so you can explain that you are not trying to be difficult, but you have a legitimate concern about releasing personal information until you are hired. Ask if they will supply you a tracking number to use. Most will. If they won't...once again, your call: play or pass.

The reason for requesting a Social Security number is usually for use by the company's internal applicant tracking system that was discussed in Chapter 4, and an alternative number should be provided to you.

STATING YOUR SALARY REQUIREMENTS ONLINE

The other field you should handle with care is "Salary Requirement." If the field will accept non-numeric characters, type in "open" or "negotiable," although only if you mean it.

These are terms that indicate you are willing to discuss a fair wage for your employment and perhaps make some trade-offs such as accepting a lower salary for a better benefits package or a more flexible work schedule.

But as with the Social Security field, you application will likely be rejected for submission without a number entry, so consider it carefully. If it takes $75,000 a year to support your home and family and you will not settle for less, don't type in $49,000. It may mean you won't be asked to interview, but at least you will not have wasted the company's time and your own.

If you really are flexible on salary, but don't know what the job is worth, you should at least have in mind the absolute bottom line number that you can accept and be happy - happy being a relative term that includes the ability to support your family, meet your obligations, and feel good about going to work on Monday morning.

The "Monday morning" standard is what I have been suggesting in my presentation for several years now. If you can pay all the bills on your current pay but have nothing left over after paying those bills, you haven't met my "Monday morning" standard. It says that after all bills are paid you are able to have fun (no matter how you define 'fun') and only then will you be good to go come Monday AM. If you have no other guidance, use this one. *That* is the number you will put in the salary range—the one that will allow you to pay *you* for working as well!

Know that the department manager, hiring manager and human resources managers all know the dollar value of the job (even if it is just a budget number) so you should have a 'working' number in mind. You can find it on the internet by searching for "salary calculator" and "cost of living comparison" (include the word comparison and use the quotation marks as shown). The results will direct you to websites that will help you determine the average salary for your type of job in your part of the country and beyond.

Armed with that information, you can enter a salary figure that you can feel confident is within the range the company is willing to pay and around which they are prepared to negotiate up or down depending on the value you have stated you will bring to the company. (**Make you money/Save you money.**)

***

In addition to including the statements mentioned in the beginning of this chapter in the "Other Comments" field, you can also discuss your reasoning behind the information you may have placed in the Social Security field (if accepted) and the Salary fields. Most of all, don't forget an all-important statement, the entire reason you are filling in the form: ask for the interview. (Thought I was going to say something else there, huh?)

Through four or more chapters of instruction in this book you've worked hard on your resume and it is now, by far, the best way to present yourself on paper to a potential employer. But if the online application is the only way the company allows employment communication, these tips will help you get the interview.

☆☆☆☆☆☆☆

REALLY Useful Job Search Tactic #37:

APPROACH THE ONLINE EMPLOYMENT APPLICATION WITH THE SAME CONFIDENCE AND KNOWLEDGE YOU APPLY TO YOUR SUPERIOR RESUME.

SOME THOUGHTS ON
THE HUMAN RESOURCES DEPARTMENT
(Once Again, For The Record, I Have Never Worked In Human Resources)

"The caterpillar does all the work
but the butterfly gets all the publicity."
- George Carlin

As a job seeker, there are some dynamics of the Human Resources (HR) department that I think you should know about. The HR department is overworked, underpaid and understaffed. That about sums it up.

During good times, the HR department will never have enough people to accomplish all the duties they are tasked with and during bad times they are the first to be pared down to skeleton staff. I have personally seen this happen far too often.

The reason is very simple, the HR department neither makes money nor saves money for the company. They can't! They don't generate revenue per se (more on this later) but by the very nature of their mission, they have to spend money.

LEAVE HR ALONE!

How is this going to help you find a job? Simple. Contact the hiring manager for the department you want to work for or contact the VP of Manufacturing, Director of Information Technology, the CEO even— but, unless you are seeking a position in HR—leave HR alone!

A regular day for HR will include such things as writing and modifying the company policy manual, monitoring benefits costs, new employee orientation and training, payroll services.

And then their might be the Department of Labor audit due today, a previous employee has just filed a harassment complaint and all records for that person must be located (for the last twelve years!) because legal just called and depositions begin at 3 this afternoon.

On top of this is the service that HR must provide to their clients— the company's employees! All the daily, mundane details of corporate life end up in HR. Details that are critical to the lives of employees.

"My check was off $723."

"Who is going to help me relocate to Des Moines?"

"My insurance hasn't activated yet!"

"My vacation days are out of line."

OK. So they are busy. Did I just happen to mention the salespeople calling with the latest, greatest employment website, the vendors trying to get an appointment to get the insurance/401K/benefits business, the corporate apartment salespeople trying to get in the door, the software implementation people that just showed up to install the applicant tracking software? It goes on and on. Everyday.

Oh yeah, and then they still have to recruit and hire 24 people this week for positions that must be filled by next Wednesday.

***

PUT ME IN, COACH!

I love the HR department. They are the assistant coaches to the CEO. They field the team. They monitor the depth and quality of the players. They *know* the players, each and every one of them. Accounting might know a lot of them. Marketing surely won't. Many times the CEO *can't* know all the players—he will defer to HR.

Recognize that HR *does not* get the appropriate recognition when *they* had the gut feel to move someone on to a hiring manager that the hiring manager may have passed on their own—and that person became the individual that devised a new method of manufacturing that brought in $220,000,000 last year! Think the pat on the back goes to HR? Not a chance.

* * *

REVERSE NETWORKING

So now here you are, a REALLY Useful Job Search candidate. How are you going to get yourself recognized so you can get some of HR's valuable time? *You don't.*

What you do is hold off submitting your resume - just for a day or so - in the manner prescribed in that *Brand New* job posting, but instead attempt to make contact with the department hiring manager that provided HR with the request to fill the open position. How do you do this? Read Chapter 10 once again for phone pointers. Now, reach out to the hiring manager acting as if you have no idea your *perfect* listing is sitting on the company website. This will take some effort but if successful, you will really be pleased with the result. (And, if you can't get through to your target hiring manager, submit your Superior Resume in the manner asked for in the posting.)

Do you recognize what has happened? You are back to networking—only kind of sideways and in reverse. Of course you already know networking is how 60-80% of all jobs are filled. The only difference this time is that you are now attempting to network for a job that you *know* is posted. Pursue it aggressively but when you get there, act like you had *no idea* your ideal opening was posted on the company website!

☆☆☆☆☆☆☆

REALLY Useful Job Search Tactics # 39:

LEAVE HR ALONE. GO DIRECTLY TO THE DEPARTMENT YOU
WANT TO WORK FOR AND DISCUSS THE OPPORTUNITY WITH
THE HIRING MANAGER OR DEPARTMENT HEAD (YOUR FUTURE
SUPERVISOR)!

REALLY Useful Job Search Tactics #40:

CONSIDER LEARNING THE REVERSE NETWORKING TECHNIQUE
AND APPLY IT TO *BRAND NEW* POSTINGS IMMEDIATELY.

CLOSING THOUGHTS

*"Find a job you like and you add
five days to every week."*

- H. Jackson Brown, Jr.

I invite you to come see me speak if I'm in your "neighborhood" and you are available to spend 2 or 3 hours with me.

I am *very* passionate about my REALLY Useful Job Search Tactics. I am *very* passionate about you creating the most compelling Superior Resume you can. (I want you to be successful doing exactly what you want to do!)

I tell you this because I must forewarn you that sometimes I will get so excited presenting my message that I have to stop and take a breath! But I'm getting better – at breathing – not toning it down!

It makes no difference to me if you are a passive or active job seeker (whether you currently have a job or not). Your age and circumstances make no difference to me. I have spoken to groups of job seekers searching for $200,000 - $600,000 annual salaried positions as well as at shelters for abused women. I am absolutely colorblind to my audience. I want my information out on the street where it will do the most good. I am most proud of the idea that everything I present in this book, on my radio show, and in person is information and tactics that you can apply to your personal job search today!

TAKE CARE OF YOURSELF

If you are currently unemployed, take time each day to get up a little earlier than you might normally and walk the block, ride a bike, swim...I don't care what you do, but do something only for you. I want you to have some "alone time" where you are in control of your situation. When the phone rings and it's a recruiter, I want you to respond with your natural vitality and energy. World news, 3 cups of coffee and 2 cigarettes before 8AM won't do the trick! A short jog around the block can make all the difference.

Don't forget those around you. If you are unemployed, your not working affects them as well. Getting some exercise is good for you and how you relate to those around you. Take care of those who take care of you.

I sincerely wish you the very best in your job search. Be compelling. Speak my your mantra: **I am here to make you money or save you money.**
And say it with conviction!

Once again and always: To your success!

Rick Gillis

THANK YOU

It seems to me that someone who writes a book this small should not have a lot of people to thank. Nothing could be further from the truth.

Steve and Manon Carr. As the owners of HoustonJOBS.com they allowed me to represent them, supported me and maybe most importantly, Steve suggested, "maybe I should write a book".

Ryan Murphy and Jerry Kowalchik who created HoustonEmployment.com of which I became employee #1. Because of this association I was exposed to what has become my calling: the Internet, human resources, staffing, job seekers, public speaking and now, talk radio.

Pastor Roy Farmer and the entire Between Jobs Ministry (Ed Bacon, Paul Cuneo, Jim Moore, and so many more!) at Northwest Bible Church in Spring, TX. BJM asked me to speak to jobseekers several years ago and has allowed me to develop my message and as a direct result, the book you hold in your hands.

Terry Atkinson, as a career & life coach, has honed her skills even further by listening and offering particularly relevant advice during my writing and editing of REALLY Useful Job Search Tactics.

Katherine Ellis who offered insightful advice during the original draft of Guerilla Job Search Tactics, the original working title of REALLY Useful Job Search Tactics.

Deborah Kreichbaum who by proofing and correcting my "obvious" mistakes makes me look better than I otherwise would.

Sue Collard, advertising agency owner, and Karen Chang, artist, who, without hesitation, jumped right in when I needed artwork.

Robin Kessler, author of <u>Competency Based Resumes</u> and <u>Competency Based Interviews</u> who has advised me every step of the way. Now that I am finished with my book, I can *finally* read hers.

Russell Smeed, my friend and sounding board. I have always said that

Russell "runs deep". Russell does not say a lot. But when he does—pay attention. It will be well worth your time.

Susanne Rothschild who is singularly one of the most positive, uplifting individuals I know. She believes in everybody! What a gift!

The wonderful R & B, who is significantly responsible for some part of virtually every chapter. This is my only way of acknowledging my gratitude. (Mysterious, huh?)

Margo and Fred Costello who told me flatly that it was time for me to do my own thing.

The corporate offices of Carlton Staffing, Houston, TX: Dave Curran, President, Lauren Terbreuggen, Marketing Manager and Cindy Jennings, Business Development Director for believing in me and supporting my concept for creating an employment based talk radio show.

Pam (J) Kelly, who as my radio show co-host, writer and producer puts her whole heart and soul into our projects.

Aric and Tory Gillis because they are my kids and I dig 'em! Aric has been in support of this project since I first mentioned it and has been wandering the bookstores of NYC searching out employment related "stuff" I should be aware of. And Tory, another person who "runs deep". Tory helps me find the right words when I'm mentally blocked. What a cool kid/young man!

I genuinely thank all the Human Resource professionals, particularly Valencia Amenson, in the greater Houston area who have allowed me into their offices since 1997 and by doing so have taught me so much. You have no idea how much I learned by just being in your presence.

I thank all the jobseekers that have given their time to listen to me. While allowing me to "tell you stuff" you have taught me much. I wish each and every one of you the very, very best. Like I say at the end of each live presentation: I hope I never see you again--unless it's in the grocery store! Success to each of you.

And lastly, but only by choice because she absolutely comes first, my